Delivering Project Excellence with the Statement of Work

Delivering Project Excellence with the Statement of Work

Michael G. Martin

MANAGEMENTCONCEPTS

Vienna, Virginia

ſſſ
MANAGEMENTCONCEPTS
8230 Leesburg Pike, Suite 800
Vienna, VA 22182
(703) 790-9595
Fax: (703) 790-1371
www.managementconcepts.com

Printed in the United States of America

Library of Congress Cataloging-in-Publication Data

Martin, Michael G., 1961–
   Delivering project excellence with the statement of work / Michael G. Martin.
     p. cm.
   Includes bibliographical references and index.
   ISBN 1-56726-113-2 (hc.)
     1. Proposal writing in business. 2. Proposal writing in public contracting.
   3. Contracts for work and labor. 4. Project management. I. Title.

HF5718.5 .M37 2002
651.7'8—dc21

                                          2002026520

About the Author

Michael G. Martin, PMP, has more than 16 years of program and project management experience in the information technology and construction industries. During his career he has been instrumental in helping organizations in both the public and private sectors achieve excellence in program and project management worldwide. A certified project management professional, he has authored or coauthored numerous articles and papers on project management. He is the past chair of the PMI® Georgia chapter and is currently a member of the PMI® Research Membership Advisory Group.

Mike holds an MBA from the University of North Florida and a BS in Civil Engineering from West Virginia Tech. He is a frequent speaker to professional organizations, companies, and universities.

Mike resides in Lawrenceville, Georgia, with his wife and two sons. To contact him, send an e-mail to: Michael.Martin@SOW-Solutions.com.

Dedication

To my Mom and Dad for teaching me the importance of hard work and perseverance. I am very thankful and blessed to have them as parents.

Table of Contents

Part 4: Changing the Paradigm **221**

**Chapter 10. Selling the Importance and
Benefits of the SOW** **223**

Index **233**

List of Figures

Foreword

In the last several years we have seen a steady flow of new books published on project management. All too often these books have drawn heavily on the existing literature and have reviewed topics that have already been treated. Unfortunately, few of these books have brought forth any new ideas or concepts that get to the heart of why projects fail—and how to make them succeed.

Mike Martin's *Delivering Project Excellence with the Statement of Work* is a refreshing exception. Instead of following the prevailing practice of paraphrasing existing books, he provides a comprehensive yet succinct description of how the statement of work (SOW) is important in setting standards for the effective management of projects. He addresses head-on the fundamental problems organizations run into when they take on a project: lack of clear, specific, and detailed requirements; absence of a change management process; and the failure to coordinate the goals of cross-functional groups within the organization and with the client organization. Not only does *Delivering Project Excellence* address these problems, but it provides a structural solution that is sensible and tangible.

This book is one that executives, project managers, and all other key stakeholders must read. It provides a process that, when adopted, will result in more successful projects and more successful organizations. Developing and applying the statement of work will yield measurable benefits. The book shows how the SOW can be used to provide the foundation of a successful project—one that satisfies the client and is profitable for the company. It also explains how to create and maintain an SOW. Moreover, *Delivering Project Excellence* provides guidance on how to sell the SOW to key project stakeholders. The concepts and processes introduced here serve as a model for managing a project to meet the expectations of both the customer and the service provider.

I believe this book to be the first of its kind. It will make a singular and significant contribution to the growing project management literature and to executives, project managers, and stakeholders who daily face the consequences of poor coordination in the selection, planning, and management of projects.

There are many choices of project management books for the manager's bookshelf. For key project stakeholders who are looking for an approach that supports project excellence, this is a book they cannot afford to be without!

Dr. David I. Cleland
Professor Emeritus
School of Engineering
University of Pittsburgh

Preface

I t is often said that "Necessity is the mother of invention." In today's competitive marketplace, it is a necessity for businesses to deliver successful projects if they want to remain viable. This is especially true in the professional services industry and in particular the information technology (IT) sector. According to research published by the Standish Group in 1999, U.S. companies lose approximately $75 billion annually on failed or mismanaged IT projects—specifically, software development projects. This figure is for the IT sector alone. It doesn't include the money lost on failed or mismanaged projects in other sectors such as telecommunications, construction, and pharmaceuticals. If we were to combine the failed projects from all of these industries, the amount of money wasted each year could easily reach into the trillions of dollars. As a result, organizations are looking for ways to manage projects more efficiently, productively, and creatively.

One of the creative methods being applied in the private sector is the statement of work (SOW). The SOW historically had been used primarily in the government contracting arena as part of the procurement process. In recent years the private sector has recognized the need for and importance of this document for planning and managing projects. Nonetheless, there is a void in the private sector regarding how to develop and apply an SOW on projects. The purpose of this book is to fill that void by establishing a baseline that organizations can use for developing detailed, quality SOWs for their projects—and thereby ensuring the success and excellence of those projects.

THE VALUE OF THE SOW

I have had the opportunity to work with many different organizations in both the private and public sectors during my career. Over the years, I've seen organizations use many different methods for trying to manage their projects. Some methods were successful, and some were not. In my personal experience and research of various organizations, the SOW was the one common factor that invariably rose to the top of the list in importance for ensuring project success. Regardless of whether the work was internal or external to the organization, without an SOW describing in detail the work to be provided, it was impossible to deliver projects on time, within budget, and of the scope and quality desired by the client. In turn, without a detailed baseline description, it was impossible to manage changes that occurred on the project during execution. This lack of a detailed description and change management process typically led to schedule delays and cost overruns, which ultimately led to project failure.

I have had the opportunity to personally witness the benefits and positive impact that an SOW can have on a project and an organization. One company I'm familiar with was losing approximately $50,000 per month providing IT support services to a client. Although an SOW type of document had been done for the project, it was poorly written and very broad in its definition of the work to be performed. It consisted of only five pages, four of which addressed the roles and responsibilities of the individual team members and stakeholders; only one page addressed the work to be performed. The service provider was reaching the point of having to make a decision whether to withdraw from the contract and cut its losses or to try to renegotiate the contract. The customer was also unhappy, as you might expect, with the level of service that it was receiving. However, the customer was willing to renegotiate the contract with the service provider and revise the SOW.

The SOW was ultimately redrafted and expanded from five pages to more than 50 pages. The revised version was very detailed and specific regarding the services to be provided to the customer, as well as the service provider's requirements to be able to deliver the stated services properly. This project was ultimately turned around and soon became profitable for the service provider, bringing in more than 30 percent gross profit. The client satisfaction ratings also improved significantly.

WHO WILL BENEFIT FROM THIS BOOK?

Although this book focuses on the professional services industry, the guidelines and processes presented can be applied to any industry and organization. Four groups make up the primary audience:

- Executive leadership
- Project managers
- Project team members
- Clients.

Individuals who make up each of these groups play an important role in the development and application of the SOW. Each group is focused on different aspects of the project and, in turn, will gain different benefits from this book. For instance, executive leadership, which is the group that must ultimately approve the SOW, will gain an understanding of the role of the SOW and its importance in increasing the likelihood of project excellence and success. The project manager, as the key facilitator or coordinator of SOW development, will need to understand every aspect of both how the SOW is developed and how it is used to manage projects during execution. Project team members can gain great value by understanding how the SOW specifically identifies their individual roles and responsibilities for the work to be performed.

Last, but not least, is the client audience. Clients who are receiving professional services will be able to use this information to document and structure their contracts to ensure that any future engagements are supported by a detailed SOW that clearly documents their requirements and the specifications of the product or service they are requesting. This should lead to more successful projects and higher satisfaction with the services they are receiving.

STRUCTURE OF THE BOOK

Four main areas are critical for an individual or organization in developing and applying an SOW effectively to a project:

1. Understanding the fundamentals of the statement of work
2. Building the statement of work
3. Maintaining the SOW for project excellence
4. Changing the paradigm.

The book is organized into these four parts to provide a roadmap that takes the reader on a journey from learning what an SOW is, to how it's developed and used on a project, to how to communicate and sell the importance of the SOW to the client as well as to your own organization. The following chapters support these four areas:

Part 1: Understanding the Fundamentals of the Statement of Work

Chapter 1—Defining the Statement of Work: This chapter provides a historical overview and definition of the SOW. The discussion addresses the evolution of the SOW from primarily a government contracting document to its newfound role in project management in the private sector. The chapter includes a rare copy of a general requirements document from the early 1900s for the Wright Brothers' heavier-than-air flying machine.

Chapter 2—The Importance of the SOW in Managing Projects: This discussion includes various case studies and real-life analogies that demonstrate the importance of the SOW in successfully delivering projects. The chapter addresses research from the Standish Group's *Chaos Report,* which identifies three primary reasons for failed and challenged projects: lack of user input, incomplete requirements and specifications, and changing requirements and specifications. All three of these factors can be attributed to the absence of a detailed SOW. The chapter concludes with a discussion of nine key benefits of having an SOW.

Chapter 3—When to Do an SOW: This chapter addresses when the SOW should be developed in both competitive and noncompetitive bidding situations. It also addresses the two types of SOW used in the private sector: the proposal SOW (PSOW) and the contract SOW (CSOW). Included in the chapter is a detailed set of guidelines on when the PSOW and CSOW apply in competitive and noncompetitive bidding situations.

Chapter 4—Who Should Develop the SOW: Forming a team of subject matter experts (SMEs) for developing the SOW is critical to ensuring that the document is of the highest quality possible. This chapter discusses how to form a TIGER (**T**otally **I**ntegrated **G**roup of **E**xpert **R**esources) team for the development of the SOW and how to build cohesiveness among the team members to ensure that they have a common vision and understanding of the project.

Part 2: Building the Statement of Work

Chapter 5—Building the SOW Foundation: This chapter introduces the methodology for developing the SOW, which consists of three simple phases: *Foundation*, *Framing*, and *Finalizing* the SOW. The chapter deals with the first phase of the F3 methodology, building the *foundation* of the SOW. This phase consists of two parts: performing a due diligence analysis and developing a work breakdown structure (WBS).

Chapter 6—Framing the SOW: *Framing* the SOW is the second step of the *F3 methodology* for building the foundation for successful projects. This step plays an important role in building consistency and improving the quality of SOWs developed in an organization. This chapter provides guidance on how to develop the structure properly as well as a detailed description of the key elements that make up the baseline framework.

Chapter 7—Finalizing the SOW: This chapter addresses the third and final phase of the *F3 methodology*, the *finalizing* phase. Included are guidelines to help the development team ensure that the document is technically and grammatically sound. The chapter also addresses the role of the SOW in pricing a project and as a supporting document to the contract. Guidelines and a checklist for ensuring that the SOW is reviewed properly are also included.

Chapter 8—Sample SOWs: The Good, the Bad, and the Downright Ugly: This chapter applies the guidelines and processes discussed in Chapters 5, 6, and 7 to develop an SOW for both a complex and a simple project. The SOW for the complex project is based on a fictitious IT outsourcing project that is delivering help desk, hardware support, and software support outsourcing services to a large telecommunications organization. The simple project examines a sample SOW for performing a project management maturity analysis on an organization with approximately 100 employees. These examples provide an overview of the type of information and the level of detail that should go into drafting an SOW.

Part 3: Maintaining the SOW for Project Excellence

Chapter 9—Managing Change to the SOW: This chapter provides an overview of why change management is important on projects, how to identify when a change occurs using the SOW, and what factors to consider that could impede the acceptance and application of a change management process in an organization. It then focuses on the change order request form and the SOW change order tracker, both of which play a critical role in successfully managing project change.

Part 4: Changing the Paradigm

Chapter 10—Selling the Importance and Benefits of the SOW: This chapter discusses how to communicate the importance of the SOW to your client as well as to your own organization. It also contains a brief discussion on how to sell the SOW as a service offering and how to use the document to sell additional services.

This book is a culmination of many years of research and experience in the development and application of SOWs in managing projects. I sincerely hope that each individual and organization that applies these concepts and techniques will realize significant benefits and improvements on their projects. I am very interested in hearing about any success stories that have come about after applying these concepts on your projects. Please feel free to e-mail these stories to me. I wish each of you much success. God bless!

Michael G. Martin, PMP
Michael.Martin@SOW-Solutions.com

Acknowledgments

I first want to thank God for providing me with the words, knowledge, and motivation to complete this book. Without His divine support this would not have been possible. Second only to God is the thanks that must go to my wife Lori and my boys Taylor and Garrett for their support and patience with me throughout these many months of writing. I am so blessed to have them for a family.

A heartfelt thanks to Cathy Kreyche, New Product Development Editor with Management Concepts, not only for proposing this much-needed text, but also for her encouragement, guidance, and the countless hours of time she spent reviewing these materials. I am deeply grateful.

A special thanks to Dr. David Cleland, Dr. Janice Thomas, Mr. Neal Whitten, and Ms. Kathy Robison for their willingness to review this manuscript. I am both deeply grateful and honored to have such a distinguished group of professionals as my reviewers. Special thanks also to my brother-in-law Michael Weeks, D.Phil. student at Oxford University, for his time and effort in researching materials for me on more than one occasion.

Part 1

Understanding the Fundamentals of the Statement of Work

I f you were asked what document or tool in your project management toolkit is most important for ensuring the successful completion and delivery of a project, what would your answer be? Would it be the project charter or the work breakdown structure (WBS)? The project plan or the schedule? A customized project management software package? An argument can be made for each of these. However, the true litmus test in determining the importance of each of these tools is to answer the question: If they weren't used, would it make a difference in the outcome of the project? Each of these can contribute to the success of the project, but they are secondary to the one document that establishes the contractual foundation of the project. That document is the statement of work (SOW).

The SOW is the most important document you will ever have on a project in that it establishes the contractual foundation upon which the project will be managed. In fact, the SOW can play a critical role in the proposal process even before a work effort is recognized as a project. What makes the SOW so important in the management of a project? It provides the project team with a clear vision of the scope and objectives of what they are to achieve.

Of the other tools, the one that comes closest in importance to the SOW is the work breakdown structure. As you'll see in Chapter 5, the WBS plays an extremely important role in developing the SOW. However, the WBS does not carry with it the contractual obligation that the SOW does. If the SOW is the contractual foundation of a project, and this foundation is, figuratively speaking, made of concrete, then the WBS is the aggregate that helps make up and hold together the concrete foundation. As for the other project management tools, if the objectives and the scope of work to be performed are unknown or not clearly defined, then the project team will not have a clear understanding of what they are to do. In turn, developing a detailed project plan, schedule, or any other document based on an unknown scope is pointless.

Chapter 1

Defining the Statement of Work

Recognizing what we have done in the past is a recognition of ourselves. By conducting a dialogue with our past, we are searching how to go forward.
—Kiyoko Takeda

B ecause so little has been written on statements of work, the SOW is defined, interpreted, and used differently in different industry sectors and organizations. Its use and application can even vary internally within an immature organization. For that reason, it is important to establish a common definition and understanding of the SOW, as well as to gain a historical perspective of what the SOW is and how it came to be used in industry.

HISTORICAL PERSPECTIVE ON THE SOW

It is said that "Necessity is the mother of invention." The necessity for businesses today is to deliver successful projects, particularly when the organization is publicly traded and the leadership has to answer to the stockholders. Thus, it is imperative that better, more efficient, and more productive ways to manage projects successfully be developed. In developing a new or improved approach to managing projects, it is valuable to first study how a concept originated and what generated the original need.

When I started researching the history of SOWs, one of the questions I set out to answer was, "Who was the first person or group to develop the document, and for what purpose?" In other words, who was that one person working late into the evening on a troubled project who decided that there needed to be a better way of formally documenting the requirements for the work to be performed? Although I was unable to find one person responsible for developing the SOW, I did uncover some interesting tidbits that have ultimately led to the document we know today as the SOW.

SOWs of the Past

One of the earliest recorded events that described the requirements of a product or service to be provided occurred several thousand years ago. These instructions described a product to be built that was of such magnitude that it ensured the continued existence of the human race. In fact, it may have been the first major engineering achievement ever undertaken by man. The product I'm referring to was the ark built by Noah around 4000 BC.[1] The description and specifications, issued by God, informed Noah of the dimensions of the ark, how to build it, and who was to be housed in its confines. The description of the ark can be found in the Bible in the Book of Genesis, Chapter 6, verses 14–21:

> So make yourself an ark of cypress wood; make rooms in it and coat it with pitch inside and out. This is how you are to build it. The ark is to be 450 feet long, 75 feet wide and 45 feet high. Make a roof for it and finish the ark to within 18 inches of the top. Put a door in the side of the ark and make lower, middle and upper decks. . . .Two of every kind of bird, of every kind of animal and of every kind of creature that moves along the ground will come to you to be kept alive. You are to take every kind of food that is to be eaten and store it away as food for you and for them.[2]

Although succinct, these specifications provided Noah with enough information to build a vessel of sufficient scale to harbor him, his family, and the creatures of earth during that time, and thereby ensured the survival of the human and animal kingdoms. Although God didn't call these instructions an SOW, they provided, at least at a high level, the type of information contained in the SOWs that we use today.

The earliest use of a formal SOW type of document in modern history appears to have occurred in the early twentieth century, when it was used primarily in government contracting. In 1908, the U.S. Army Signal Corps drafted a general requirements document to identify the required specifications of the Wright Brothers' heavier-than-air flying machine (see Figure 1-1). This document was approximately

Figure 1-1. General Requirements Document and Contract for Wright Brothers' Heavier-then-Air Flying Machine

SIGNAL CORPS SPECIFICATION, NO. 486.

ADVERTISEMENT AND SPECIFICATION FOR A HEAVIER-THAN-AIR FLYING MACHINE.

To THE PUBLIC:

Sealed proposals, in duplicate, will be received at this office until 12 o'clock noon on February 1, 1908, on behalf of the Board of Ordnance and Fortification for furnishing the Signal Corps with a heavier-than-air flying machine. All proposals received will be turned over to the Board of Ordnance and Fortification at its first meeting after February 1 for its official action.

Persons wishing to submit proposals under this specification can obtain the necessary forms and envelopes by application to the Chief Signal Officer, United States Army, War Department, Washington, D. C. The United States reserves the right to reject any and all proposals.

Unless the bidders are also the manufacturers of the flying machine they must state the name and place of the maker.

Preliminary.—This specification covers the construction of a flying machine supported entirely by the dynamic reaction of the atmosphere and having no gas bag.

Acceptance.—The flying machine will be accepted only after a successful trial flight, during which it will comply with all requirements of this specification. No payments on account will be made until after the trial flight and acceptance.

Inspection.—The Government reserves the right to inspect any and all processes of manufacture.

GENERAL REQUIREMENTS.

The general dimensions of the flying machine will be determined by the manufacturer, subject to the following conditions:

1. Bidders must submit with their proposals the following:
   (a) Drawings to scale showing the general dimensions and shape of the flying machine which they propose to build under this specification.
   (b) Statement of the speed for which it is designed.
   (c) Statement of the total surface area of the supporting planes.
   (d) Statement of the total weight.
   (e) Description of the engine which will be used for motive power.
   (f) The material of which the frame, planes, and propellers will be constructed. Plans received will not be shown to other bidders.

2. It is desirable that the flying machine should be designed so that it may be quickly and easily assembled and taken apart and packed for transportation in army wagons. It should be capable of being assembled and put in operating condition in about one hour.

3. The flying machine must be designed to carry two persons having a combined weight of about 350 pounds, also sufficient fuel for a flight of 125 miles.

4. The flying machine should be designed to have a speed of at least forty miles per hour in still air, but bidders must submit quotations in their proposals for cost depending upon the speed attained during the trial flight, according to the following scale:

   40 miles per hour, 100 per cent.
   39 miles per hour, 90 per cent.
   38 miles per hour, 80 per cent.
   37 miles per hour, 70 per cent.
   36 miles per hour, 60 per cent.
   Less than 36 miles per hour rejected.
   41 miles per hour, 110 per cent.
   42 miles per hour, 120 per cent.
   43 miles per hour, 130 per cent.
   44 miles per hour, 140 per cent.

5. The speed accomplished during the trial flight will be determined by taking an average of the time over a measured course of more than five miles, against and with the wind. The time will be taken by a flying start, passing the starting point at full speed at both ends of the course. This test subject to such additional details as the Chief Signal Officer of the Army may prescribe at the time.

6. Before acceptance a trial endurance flight will be required of at least one hour during which time the flying machine must remain continuously in the air without landing. It shall return to the starting point and land without any damage that would prevent it immediately starting upon another flight. During this trial flight of one hour it must be steered in all directions without difficulty and at all times under perfect control and equilibrium.

7. Three trials will be allowed for speed as provided for in paragraphs 4 and 5. Three trials for endurance as provided for in paragraph 6, and both tests must be completed within a period of thirty days from the date of delivery. The expense of the tests to be borne by the manufacturer. The place of delivery to the Government and trial flights will be at Fort Myer, Virginia.

8. It should be so designed as to ascend in any country which may be encountered in field service. The starting device must be simple and transportable. It should also land in a field without requiring a specially prepared spot and without damaging its structure.

9. It should be provided with some device to permit of a safe descent in case of an accident to the propelling machinery.

10. It should be sufficiently simple in its construction and operation to permit an intelligent man to become proficient in its use within a reasonable length of time.

11. Bidders must furnish evidence that the Government of the United States has the lawful right to use all patented devices or appurtenances which may be a part of the flying machine, and that the manufacturers of the flying machine are authorized to convey the same to the Government. This refers to the unrestricted right to use the flying machine sold to the Government, but does not contemplate the exclusive purchase of patent rights for duplicating the flying machine.

12. Bidders will be required to furnish with their proposal a certified check amounting to ten per cent of the price stated for the 40-mile speed. Upon making the award for this flying machine these certified checks will be returned to the bidders, and the successful bidder will be required to furnish a bond, according to Army Regulations, of the amount equal to the price stated for the 40-mile speed.

13. The price quoted in proposals must be understood to include the instruction of two men in the handling and operation of this flying machine. No extra charge for this service will be allowed.

14. Bidders must state the time which will be required for delivery after receipt of order.

JAMES ALLEN,
Brigadier General, Chief Signal Officer of the Army.

SIGNAL OFFICE,
WASHINGTON, D. C., *December 23, 1907.*

Form No. 18.

Signal Corps, United States Army.

These Articles of Agreement entered into this --------**tenth**--------- day of

February---, nineteen hundred and-**eight**--, between ----**Chas. S. Wallace**----, **Captain**------------------, Signal Corps, United States Army, of the first part, and

Wilbur and Orville Wright, trading as Wright Brothers, of 1127 West Third Street, Dayton,

in the county of--------**Montgomery**----------, State of------**Ohio**----------- of the second part, WITNESSETH, that in conformity with copy of the advertisement, specifications, and proposal hereunto attached, and which, in so far as they relate to this contract, form a part of it, the said------------------**Chas. S. Wallace, Captain,**------------------ Signal Corps, United States Army, for and in behalf of the United States of America, and the said --------------------------**Wright Brothers**-------------------------- (hereinafter designated as the contractor) do covenant and agree, to and with each other, as follows, viz:

ARTICLE I. That the said contractor shall **manufacture for and deliver to the United States of America,**

One (1) heavier-than-air flying machine, in accordance with Signal Corps Specification No. 486, dated December 23, 1907.

ART. II. That the deliveries of the supplies and materials herein contracted for shall be made in the manner, numbers, or quantities, and for each number or quantity, on or before the date specified therefor, as follows, viz:

That complete delivery shall be made on or before August 28, 1908.

ART. III. All supplies and materials furnished and work done under this contract shall, before being accepted, be subject to a rigid inspection by an inspector appointed on the part of the Government,

5—1180

and such as do not conform to the specifications set forth in this contract shall be rejected. The decision of the Chief Signal Officer, United States Army, as to quality and quantity shall be final.

ART. IV. That for and in consideration of the faithful performance of the stipulations of this contract, the contractor shall be paid at the office of -----**the Chief Signal Officer**---- ----------**of the Army**---------, at-----**Washington, D. C.**---, for all supplies and materials delivered in conformity with the requirements of this contract, on or before the dates above specified (Article II, *supra*) *and accepted*, the following prices, viz:

One (1) heavier-than-air flying machine at a total cost of twenty-five thousand (25,000) dollars.

to be paid as soon as practicable after the acceptance of the same, in funds furnished by the United States for the purpose, reserving per cent from each payment until final settlement, on completion of the contract or otherwise.

ART. V. It is further agreed that for all supplies and materials which shall not be delivered in conformity with the requirements of this contract on or before the dates prescribed therefor in Article II, above, but which shall be subsequently delivered and accepted, the prices shall be as follows:

5—1180

Figure 1-1. General Requirements Document and Contract for Wright Brothers' Heavier-then-Air Flying Machine (continued)

Art. VI. That in case of the ... y of the said contractor to perf ... he stipulations of this contract within the time and in the manner specified above, Articles I to III, inclusive, the said party of the first part may, instead of waiting further for deliveries under the provisions of the preceding article, supply the deficiency by purchase in open market or otherwise, at such place as may be selected (the articles so procured to be the kind herein specified, as near as practicable); and the said contractor shall be charged with the increased cost of the supplies and materials so purchased over what they would have cost if delivered by the contractor on the date they were received under such open-market purchase.

Art. VII. It is further agreed by and between the parties hereto that until final inspection and acceptance of, and payment for, all of the supplies and materials and work herein provided for, no prior inspection, payment, or act is to be construed as a waiver of the right of the party of the first part to reject any defective articles or supplies or to require the fulfillment of any of the terms of the contract.

Art. VIII. The contractor further agrees to hold and save the United States harmless from and against all and every demand, or demands, of any nature or kind for, or on account of, the use of any patented invention, article, or process included in the materials hereby agreed to be furnished and work to be done under this contract.

Art. IX. Neither this contract nor any interest herein shall be transferred to any other party or parties, and in case of such transfer the United States may refuse to carry out this contract either with the transferor or the transferee, but all rights of action for any breach of this contract by said contractor are reserved to the United States.

Art. X. No Member of or Delegate to Congress, nor any person belonging to, or employed in, the military service of the United States, is or shall be admitted to any share or part of this contract, or to any benefit which may arise therefrom.*

Art. XI. That it is expressly agreed and understood that this contract shall be noneffective until an appropriation adequate to its fulfillment is made by Congress and is available.

Art. XII. That this contract shall be subject to approval of the Chief Signal Officer, United States Army.

IN WITNESS WHEREOF the parties aforesaid have hereunto placed their hands the date first hereinbefore written.

Witnesses:

John J. Mullaney .... as to

Albert Larurere .... as to

C. E. Taylor .... as to

H. Y. Hoffman .... as to

.... Signal Corps, U. S. Army.

Wright Brothers
by Orville Wright

Approved: FEB 2 8 1908 , 190

....
Brigadier General,
Chief Signal Officer of the Army.

*Here add to any contract made with an incorporated company for its general benefit the following words, viz: "But this stipulation, so far as it relates to Members or Delegates to Congress, is not to be construed to extend to this contract." See section 3740, Revised Statutes.

(executed in quintuplicate.)

8—1369

7

one page in length and included requirements such as: ". . .be easily taken apart for transport in Army wagons and be capable of being reassembled for operation in an hour, carry 350 pounds for 125 miles, and maintain 40 miles per hour in still air."[3] Compared to SOWs used in business today, which can easily exceed 100 pages, this was a relatively simple document for a very complex product.

SOWs of the Present

Today, the government requires a much more in-depth document and description of what the SOW should look like and the level of detail that should be included. The Federal Acquisition Regulation (FAR), which is the primary regulation used by all federal executive agencies in their acquisition of supplies and services, identifies the term and use of the SOW in nine subsections.[4] In subsection 37.602-1—Statements of Work, the regulation not only defines the SOW, but also specifies how it is to be prepared. The subsection reads as follows:

(a) Generally, statements of work shall define requirements in clear, concise language identifying specific work to be accomplished. Statements of work must be individually tailored to consider the period of performance, deliverable items, if any, and the desired degree of performance flexibility (see 11.106). In the case of task order contracts, the statement of work for the basic contract need only define the scope of the overall contract (see 16.504(a)(4)(iii)). The statement of work for each task issued under a task order contract shall comply with paragraph (b) of this subsection. To achieve the maximum benefits of performance-based contracting, task order contracts should be awarded on a multiple award basis (see 16.504(c) and 16.505(b)).

(b) When preparing statements of work, agencies shall, to the maximum extent possible—

(1) Describe the work in terms of "what" is to be the required output rather than either "how" the work is to be accomplished or the number of hours to be provided (see 11.002(a)(2) and 11.101);

(2) Enable assessment of work performance against measurable performance standards;

(3) Rely on the use of measurable performance standards and financial incentives in a competitive environment to encourage

competitors to develop and institute innovative and cost-effective methods of performing the work; and

(4) Avoid combining requirements into a single acquisition that is too broad for the agency or a prospective contractor to manage effectively."[5]

In federal contracting, the SOW is of utmost importance because it is the only official description of the work requirement in the request for proposal (RFP).[6] As part of the RFP, it allows contractors competing for an award to price out their proposal properly without having to allow for a lot of unknown requirements, which in turn leads to a higher percentage of contingencies in the price. A common understanding of the work to be performed helps ensure consistency in the various contractors' submitted proposals. With a common understanding of *what* is to be provided, there are fewer discrepancies and variations between the proposals. This in turn allows reviewers to evaluate the proposals on an equal basis.

The SOW has become such a critical element of the federal procurement process that several federal agencies, including the National Aeronautics and Space Administration (NASA) and the Department of Defense (DOD), have drafted detailed guidelines that show how to prepare an SOW and how to use it in the procurement process. Today's SOWs are more extensive and detailed than that drafted for the construction of the Wright Brothers' plane. The level of detail and specificity, however, is necessary to handle the complex projects now undertaken in industry.

The complexity of projects today, particularly large technology projects, has led to the need for, and use of, SOWs not only in the government arena, but in the private sector as well. Rather than simply being a procurement document, as used in the government environment, SOWs in the private sector often serve as the contractual foundation upon which project success is measured. As such, the SOW has evolved to become a document of critical importance during the execution and delivery of a project, which the project man-

> *The complexity of projects today, particularly large technology projects, has led to the need for, and use of, SOWs not only in the government arena, but in the private sector as well.*

ager can use to ensure that the project is meeting the clients' established requirements and objectives.

For instance, let's take a quick look at how the SOW would be applied in the professional services industry. Unlike some industries, such as construction, where detailed drawings and design documents are used in determining how a product or structure is to be delivered, the professional services industry often has to describe projects in narrative form. In the past, commitments within this industry sector were often made through a verbal agreement or handshake. A contract might have been signed, but it was unlikely that there was a detailed description of the product or service to be delivered. Unfortunately, this informal approach led to many project failures.

In today's competitive environment, this informal attitude and lack of management focus on the client and the work to be performed are no longer acceptable. This is particularly true when millions of dollars are at stake on a single project that, if not successful, could jeopardize an organization's future existence. To increase the likelihood of a project's success, it is imperative for both the client and the service provider to work hand-in-hand to develop a detailed description of the work to be accomplished

> *To increase the likelihood of a project's success, it is imperative for both the client and the service provider to work hand-in-hand to develop a detailed description of the work to be accomplished that will establish a solid foundation for the project going forward.*

that will establish a solid foundation for the project going forward. It should be the one required document, in addition to the contract, on every engagement.

INDUSTRY STANDARD DEFINITION OF THE SOW

Over the years I have heard many aliases used to describe the SOW, including scope of work, needs assessment, design document, and even project charter. The frequent use of these misnomers clearly indicates a lack of project management knowledge as well as immaturity within private industry as a whole in managing projects.

By contrast, in the government contracting arena, standards for the SOW have been established, and the definition of an SOW varies only slightly across agencies. For example, DOD defines the SOW as the document that "should specify in clear, understandable terms the work to be done in developing or producing the goods to be delivered or services to be performed by a contractor." In addition, it should define "(either directly or by reference to other documents) all work (non-specification) performance requirements for contractor effort."[7] NASA defines the SOW as the document that "describes the work to be performed or the services to be rendered; defines the respective responsibilities of the Government and the contractor; serves as a basis for contractor response, evaluation of proposals and source selection; and ultimately provides an objective measure so that both the Government and the contractor will know when the work is satisfactorily completed and payment is justified."[8]

Unlike the public sector, private industry doesn't have a definition of the SOW that is used consistently within an industry, or for that matter even within an organization. The closest thing to an industry standard definition is that from the Project Management Institute's (PMI®'s) Project Management Body of Knowledge (PMBOK®). The PMBOK® defines a statement of work as "a narrative description of products or services to be supplied under contract."[9] This definition, however, is of limited use for the private sector, particularly for those in professional services. As written, it can be interpreted to mean only those products and services to be provided to the client; however, for those in professional services, it should also encompass the needs and requirements of the contractor or service provider to be able to deliver the products and services properly.

DEFINITION OF THE SOW IN THE NEW ECONOMY

As SOWs become more prevalent in industry, it becomes increasingly important that they address the responsibilities of all parties involved. Professional service providers often become so focused on identifying and defining the client's needs and requirements that they often overlook their own needs and requirements. It is imperative that the provider's needs and requirements also be met so that they can deliver a quality product or service. For example, in an outsourcing engagement, if proper facilities aren't provided to the contractor, the quality of service provided to the client will likely suffer.

I propose that the PMI® definition of the SOW be expanded to reflect the needs of private industry today and in the future. As such, my proposed revised definition reads as follows:

A narrative description of the products and services to be supplied to the client and the needs and requirements of the contractor to deliver such products and services properly under the contract.[10]

The old definition, which simply states that the document should define the products and services under contract, completely ignored the duties or obligation of the client to cooperate with the service provider and provide an acceptable environment such that the service provider can properly deliver such products or services. This revised definition better reflects the importance of the SOW from the perspectives of both the client and the service provider. Thus, it is this definition upon which the rest of this book will be based.

> The SOW has come a long way from the one-page document used to define the requirements of the Wright Brothers' heavier-than-air flying machine to arguably the most important document for delivering successful projects in today's highly competitive private sector environment. Throughout its evolution, the SOW's role and importance have expanded far beyond just being a document used in the federal procurement process. In the private sector, the SOW is used not only as a supporting document to the contract, but also as a tool for managing the project throughout its lifecycle. This new application has required that the old definition of the SOW be revised to reflect its use in today's marketplace. Expanding the definition to include not only the needs and requirements of the client, but also the needs and requirements of the team delivering the products or services, helps reflect the SOW's role in the new economy. This revised definition will in turn help organizations in all industry sectors better develop and apply SOWs to their unique environments.

NOTES

[1]Werner Keller, *The Bible As History, 2nd revised edition* (New York: William Morrow & Company, Inc., 1980).

[2]*Life Application Bible* (co-published by Zondervan Publishing House and Tyndale House Publishers, 1991).

[3]Department of Defense, *Handbook for Preparation of Statement of Work* (SOW), MIL-HDBK-245D, 3 April 1996, superseding MIL-HDBK-245C, 10 September 1991.

[4]Federal Acquisition Regulation (FAR), FAC 97-14, June 1997 edition.

[5]FAR, subsection 37.602-1—Statements of Work.

[6]Peter S. Cole, *How to Write a Statement of Work* (Vienna, VA: Management Concepts, Inc., 1999).

[7]Department of Defense, p. 6.

[8]NASA Handbook 5600.2A—*Statements of Work Handbook,* 23 July 1993.

[9]Project Management Institute, *A Guide to the Project Management Body of Knowledge (PMBOK® Guide—2000 Edition)* (Newtown Square, PA: Project Management Institute, 2000).

[10]Michael G. Martin, "Statement of Work: The Foundation for Delivering Successful Service Projects," *PM Network,* Project Management Institute, Inc. (October 1998, Vol. 12, No. 10), pp. 54-57. © 1998, Project Management Institute, Inc. All rights reserved.

Chapter 2

The Importance of the SOW in Managing Projects

Good fortune brings in some boats that are not steered. Only direction can bring in the fleet.

—William Shakespeare

Most project failures occur in the initiation and planning phases. It's during this time that the foundation for the project is established, which will ultimately determine whether the project will succeed or fail. The foundational document for managing projects is the detailed SOW. Without a detailed SOW, you're managing a project with an unknown objective. This makes it difficult to determine what is to be accomplished, when you're finished, and what method will be used for measuring the success of both you and the project. You also have no baseline against which to measure progress or change (e.g., scope, cost, schedule).

Change is inevitable regardless of how good and detailed project planning is. Change, in and of itself, will not cause a project to fail; rather, it's an organization's inability to manage change properly that will ultimately lead to its demise. In the absence of an established baseline or foundation (i.e., a SOW) for a project, you will be left trying to manage change on an undefined and unknown scope.

Change, in and of itself, will not cause a project to fail; rather, it's an organization's inability to manage change properly that will ultimately lead to its demise.

As noted in Chapter 1, we are defining the SOW as a detailed narrative description of the products and services to be delivered to a client under contract, as well as the service provider's requirements to be able to deliver the products and services properly. Having a solid foundation is an essential element for delivering project excellence.

Imagine that you're going to build your dream home. One of the first things you do in constructing the home is to lay the foundation. Since this is what the physical structure rests upon, the structural integrity of the house is largely determined by the stability of the foundation. If the foundation is unstable, then the house will be unstable. While it's possible to go back and make adjustments to the superstructure, it is often impossible to make changes or adjustments to the foundation once it's in place. Thus, it is imperative that all of the upfront planning and engineering be done correctly if the foundation is to be constructed right the first time.[1]

In the Bible, the construction of a house serves as a metaphor for building one's life on a solid foundation:

> *Therefore everyone who hears these words of mine and puts them into practice is like a wise man who built his house on the rock. The rain came down, the streams rose, and the winds blew and beat against that house; yet it did not fall, because it had its foundation on the rock. But everyone who hears these words of mine and does not put them into practice is like a foolish man who built his house on sand. The rain came down, the streams rose, and the winds blew and beat against that house, and it fell with a great crash.[2]*

If we apply this analogy to a project, the SOW would be the foundation (or rock) upon which we build out projects. When a project is entered into without a detailed SOW, it's like constructing a house upon the sand, with the end result being the same. The wind and rain would be synonymous with the scope, cost, and schedule changes that are constantly bearing down on projects. Without a detailed SOW, these changes will continue beating on the project until it is no longer manageable and it ultimately reaches a point of imminent failure. Just like the house built upon sand, the failure of a project initiated without an SOW will be great and heard throughout the organization.[3]

REASONS FOR HAVING AN SOW

Have you ever been assigned to do a task or project with very little direction regarding what to do or how to go about doing it? If so, you know that it can be a very frustrating experience. When I have the opportunity to speak on the topic of SOWs, I like to use a short role-play exercise, which I call the "toothpaste syndrome."

In setting up the exercise, I ask for a volunteer from the audience to play the role of the project manager (PM) while I play the role of the business developer. I then inform the audience that as the business developer I have recently sold an engagement to a client, which requires us to squeeze toothpaste from a tube and then reverse the process and put it back in. The project will be deemed successful if we can put all the toothpaste that has been extracted back into the tube. I also tell the audience that I've informed the client that our project manager has experience in this type of work and will have no problem delivering on this engagement.

Of course, when the volunteer PM tries to put the toothpaste back into the tube, he or she quickly finds out that it's an impossible task. People have tried many different methods to get the content back into the tube, including forming funnels and trying to squeeze the paste back in. No one has been successful yet! By not being able to put all the toothpaste back into the tube, the volunteer PM is unsuccessful, the project is deemed unsuccessful, and the client is dissatisfied. Not quite the success story you would want to submit as a best practice for your organization, is it?

In debriefing this exercise, I focus on several areas that contribute to the volunteer PM being unsuccessful. First, the scope of the work to be performed is not realistic for our team, which in this case consists solely of a volunteer PM who clearly doesn't have the skills to do the work. In addition to not having the skills, the volunteer PM doesn't have any tools available to assist in the effort. Moreover, the PM was not allowed to provide any input into whether the commitment being made to the client was realistic or not. If the PM had been consulted before the commitment was made to the client, then all of this unpleasantness would have been avoided.

When commitments are made, whether they're verbal or written, the client expects the service provider to deliver on them. If they're not met, then the client is going to be very dissatisfied. My guidance to the audience is to be very cautious about the commitments you make and ensure that you can actually deliver on them before saying you can. This is easier said than done, particularly when you have business developers whose success is measured differently from the way success is measured for the individuals actually delivering the services. Unless the performance metrics focus on the successful delivery of an engagement and they're consistent for all functions within the service provider, it will be a challenge to avoid this type of situation.

Although the "toothpaste syndrome" is fictitious, the scenario of making commitments on projects that are not clearly defined is a reality that is occurring every day in industry. Without clearly defining what work is to be provided to the customer and without having the right people defining and delivering this work, it's simply a matter of time before the project fails, if it gets off the ground at all. There's an old saying that "the road to hell is paved with good intentions." This is also true for projects, with just a slight twist: "The road to *project failure* is paved with good intentions." In the management of projects, good intentions are worthless unless they're documented and followed through on throughout the life of the project.

You don't have to look far for reasons why you need an SOW for your projects. Evidence is provided every day on the nightly news on projects that have failed or been mismanaged to the tune of millions and sometimes billions of dollars. Typically, we only hear about the projects that are politically sensitive or in the public's eye. These are only the tip of the iceberg.

You may be shocked (or you may not be) at the number of failed and challenged projects even within your own organization that you never hear about. It's these projects that are the "silent killers" of an organization. They're just like heart disease is to a human being. You think everything's fine. You've gotten a clean bill of health, and then BAM! You suffer a massive coronary. It may or may not kill you. If not, it will take you some time to recover. You then start looking for reasons why this happened even after you received a clean bill of health. Regardless of the reason, you are going to have to change your lifestyle and eating habits to prevent this from happening again.

It's the same for organizations. The financial reports may indicate that the company is in good shape and the future projections are good. Then all of a sudden several projects that were not politically sensitive or highly visible in the organization fail. The failure may or may not be significant enough to cause the overall organization to collapse. If not, it will take some time to recover and overcome these losses. The organization will start looking for reasons why the projects failed. Immediate changes will be required in the way projects are managed to prevent this from happening again. The synergy generated from the failure of this aggregate of small projects will have a much greater impact on an organization than the failure of one highly visible project. It's this type of negative impact that will ultimately cause an organization to fail.

Project failure is nondiscriminating and can occur in any industry and in any organization at any time. Reasons for failed and challenged projects include: incomplete and changing requirements, scope creep, lack of executive support, lack of skilled resources, lack of client input, changing priorities, lack of planning, unrealistic schedule, and reduced funding, just to name a few.[4] These are all valid concerns; however, I believe that the single most significant cause of project failure is the lack of a clearly defined and detailed statement of work.

One particular engagement I'm familiar with was losing approximately $50,000 per month providing IT support services to a client. The project consisted of providing support for shrink-wrapped software, network operating, and workstation operating system software and proprietary software for approximately 12,000 workstations and laptops. After a couple of months of losing significant revenue and profit, a project recovery team was called in to determine the reason for these losses and to recommend a corrective action plan.

> *The single most significant cause of project failure is the lack of a clearly defined and detailed statement of work.*

The recovery team's first step was to meet with the members of the project team and perform due diligence on the project documentation. The recovery team found that an SOW had been done for the project, but it was poorly written and very broad in its definition of the work to be performed. It consisted of only five pages, four of which addressed the roles and responsibilities of the individual team members and stakeholders; only one page addressed the work to be performed.

Poor documentation and poor writing were only two of the things wrong with this SOW. Perhaps most importantly, there was no communication between the service provider and the client during the development of the SOW. This lack of communication resulted in an SOW that did not provide a clear and detailed description of the services to be provided that was understood and agreed to by both parties.

For example, one section of the SOW stated that the service provider would provide break/fix support to the customer. The service provider intended break/fix to mean only support to hardware items, while the customer interpreted it to mean support to both hardware and software. The service provider had not staffed the engagement properly to support software calls. Thus, the technicians and help desk personnel were spending a large amount of time on calls they were not qualified to address. This resulted in significant financial penalties for not meeting the service levels agreed to for the other aspects of the project. The project was quickly becoming unprofitable. The service provider was reaching the point of having to make a decision of whether to withdraw from the contract and cut its losses or to renegotiate the contract. The customer was also unhappy. Fortunately, however, the customer was willing to renegotiate the contract and revise the SOW.

The SOW was ultimately redrafted and expanded from five pages to more than 50 pages. The revised version was very detailed and specific regarding the types of services to be provided to the customer, as well as the service provider's requirements to deliver those services properly. This project was ultimately turned around, and very soon became profitable, bringing in over 30 percent in gross profit. Most of the problems that occurred on this project could have been avoided if time had been taken upfront to plan, document, and draft a detailed SOW.

One of the most referenced reports on project failure is the *Chaos Report*, which was published by the Standish Group International in 1995. This report issued a wake-up call to the IT sector on how bad the industry was in managing projects. The findings from this report include:

- An estimated $81 billion would be spent on canceled software projects in 1995
- An estimated additional $59 billion would be paid for completed software projects in excess of their original estimates
- 41% of IT projects are canceled before completion
- 25% of all projects are canceled due to scope changes
- Less than 15% of all projects have a change management plan
- Only 16% of projects are completed on time and on budget
- 50% of all IT projects that are completed are over budget by up to 189% and contain less than 59% of the original functionality.[5]

In 1998, the Standish Group published an update to the *Chaos Report* that showed notable improvements in the success of IT projects during the five-year period since the initial research. For example, in 1994 only 16% of the projects were completed on time and within budget; by 1998 this percentage had increased to 26%.[6] The two most significant improvements were in the reduction of the cost of failed projects from $81 billion in 1995 to approximately $75 billion in 1998 and in the reduction of cost overruns from $59 billion in 1995 to $22 billion in 1998.[7] Although significant improvements were made during this five-year period, the costs of failed projects and cost overruns are still enormously high and remain the norm rather than the exception for the IT industry.

During the survey conducted for this report, participants identified three factors as the primary reasons for failed and challenged projects:

- Lack of user input
- Incomplete requirements and specifications
- Changing requirements and specifications.[8]

All three of these factors can be attributed to the absence of a detailed SOW. For instance, in order to draft a detailed SOW it is critical that the right resources participate in the process. This includes ensuring that the client is involved. (This topic is covered in more detail in Chapter 4.) A detailed description of the requirements and specifications will provide a baseline for determining when a change has occurred on the project and enable the project team to manage that change appropriately.

It is estimated that U.S. businesses and government agencies spend approximately $275 billion annually on IT projects.[9] In follow-on research conducted in 1998, the Standish Group estimated that failed and challenged projects cost these organizations approximately $97 billion annually.[10] Although this was a significant improvement from the $150 billion estimated in 1994, it is still a critical problem for the IT sector.[11] It's also important to re-emphasize that this is only for the IT sector, more specifically software development projects. This doesn't include the money lost on mismanaged telecommunications, construction, pharmaceutical projects, etc.

An example of a failed IT project occurred in 1993, when the Oregon Department of Motor Vehicles (DMV) initiated a project to computerize its paper-based records. This project was estimated to take five years and cost $50 million. Two years into the project, the scheduled completion had slipped three years, and the cost had escalated to an astounding $123 million (an increase of $73 million). A prototype of the new system was rolled out in 1996, and within a couple of days of testing there were so many complaints about the usability of the system that the decision was made to cancel the project. The failure was attributed to the lack of user input and inadequate definition of the scope of the project.[12] Millions of dollars could have been saved simply by having a detailed SOW in place.

The Oregon DMV is not the only DMV that has had problems implementing a new system. In 1987, the California DMV initiated a project to replace its mainframe system with a client/server driver's license and registration system. After six years and $45 million, it became apparent that no tangible benefits were going to be derived from the project. Thus, it was ultimately canceled in 1993. Numerous problems plagued the project from the outset; the lack of a detailed scope and objectives definition was considered to be a significant contributor to the failure.

DMVs are not the only groups that have had difficulty developing detailed SOWs on their projects. In the early 1990s, American Airlines entered into a joint venture with Budget, Hilton, and Marriott to develop and implement a new reservation system. Unfortunately, the project was initiated without having the scope clearly defined or a good change process in place. This ultimately led to the joint venture being dissolved and the project canceled—at a hefty price. It was estimated that approximately $160 million had been wasted on this project.[13,14]

Even if these three projects aren't in your particular industry, many of the lessons learned are widely applicable. As noted, project failure is not restricted to a single industry or organization. Most of the examples discussed so far have been specific to the IT industry; however, construction and other industries are not immune to project failures due to the lack of an SOW. In 1998, local trading standards departments in the United Kingdom received more than 100,000 complaints about builders being late in completing projects.[15] The lack of a detailed description of the work to be performed was cited as the primary reason for the delays. Another factor contributing to the delays was the numerous changes occurring from both the contractors and customers. Again, without a good starting baseline it becomes very difficult to determine when a change occurs, much less to measure and manage changes.

While the funds wasted on IT projects seem large, they are small in comparison to the cost overruns and funds wasted on construction projects. One of the most infamous construction projects is the "Big Dig." The Big Dig is a highway project in Boston that was initiated in 1991 to provide an underground connection between the Massachusetts Turnpike and Boston's interstates. The original estimated cost for the project was $2.6 billion. In April 2000, Federal Highway Administration (FHA) auditors were called in to investigate reports that the project had incurred significant cost overruns and was well over budget. FHA auditors estimated that the cost of the project had increased to approximately $14 billion—more than $11 billion above the original estimate.[16] This example again illustrates the importance of having a detailed SOW that clearly establishes a baseline upon which change can be determined and measured.

BENEFITS OF THE SOW

If you've ever been asked to review a failed or challenged project, and you determine that the situation could have been avoided by simply having a detailed SOW in place, then you can understand what a frustrating experience it can be. The frustration comes from realizing that millions, and possibly billions, of dollars could have been saved and the project could have been successful if only time had been taken at the outset to document properly the work to be performed. In these situations, neither the service provider nor client wins. The service provider will be losing profit, and the client will be dissatisfied because expectations are not being met.

In his book titled *Managing the Professional Service Firm*, Dr. David Maister identified what he called "The First Law of Service":[17]

SATISFACTION = PERCEPTION - EXPECTATION

In other words, if customers perceive that the level of service, or work effort, that they're receiving is less than what they originally expected, then they are going to be dissatisfied. However, if the perceived the level of service is greater than what they expected, then they'll be satisfied.[18]

The SOW is the document that will help ensure that expectations are properly established with the client and that the project team doesn't commit to performing work that they're incapable of doing. Having expectations properly established greatly increases the likelihood that the project team will deliver at least, and possibly more than, what was originally expected. This, in turn, will equate to a higher client satisfaction rating.

Caution should be exercised, however, in trying to exceed client expectations. Service providers are sometimes so focused on exceeding client expectations that they do work beyond the scope of the project. Care should be taken to ensure that if work is done on a pro bono basis, it is documented and communicated to the client. Otherwise, any work done outside of the agreed-upon scope should be handled as a change and billed appropriately.

> *The SOW is the document that will help ensure that expectations are properly established with the client and that the project team doesn't commit to performing work that they're incapable of doing.*

To visualize the importance of the SOW in customer satisfaction, consider the following scenario. The next time you start a new engagement, bring a board, a hammer, and some nails with you. Starting on day one, every time you don't achieve an established service level or the client expresses concern about the work not meeting their needs or requirements, take a nail and drive it into the board. Continue doing this until you start meeting the service levels or client satisfaction goes above a certain level. Each time this happens, remove one of the nails from the board. The goal is to get to a point where there are no nails remaining in the board.

Once all the nails have been removed, you may think that you've done an outstanding job. However, you then need to step back and take a hard look at the board that is now pockmarked and disfigured because of all of the earlier mistakes. These mistakes have tainted the appearance of the board forever. It's the same with your relationship with the client. By not having a detailed SOW initially on a project, the initial mistakes made on the project will impact and influence the client going forward.

The benefits of having a detailed SOW on your project can be enormous. They include:

Provides a basis for responding to an RFP: Often organizations are faced with having to respond to an RFP in a matter of days, with little time for planning, designing, and estimating a solution for the client. If the client has not identified a format for responding to the RFP (which is often the case in the private sector), then the SOW can be used to provide a detailed structure or framework for responding to the RFP. This structure will help the proposal team identify what specific services or products are to be provided to the client, which in turn will allow them to provide the client with the best possible estimate for performing this work.

Provides a basis for determining the price: The SOW can play an important role in determining the price for delivering a service or product to the client. Defining in detail the types of service to be provided to the client will allow the proposal team to identify any potential gaps or risks associated with delivering this work effort. In doing so, the team can provide the client with best possible estimate based on the information provided at the time of the response. (The importance of the SOW in pricing an engagement will be covered in more detail in Chapter 7.)

Provides a baseline upon which change is measured: One of the most important benefits of the SOW is using it as a baseline upon which to determine and measure change during the project. This is particularly true once the project moves into the

> *One of the most important benefits of the SOW is using it as a baseline upon which to determine and measure change during the project.*

execution or implementation phase. Without having a defined baseline upon which to measure change, a project manager would never know if a change was occurring, and it would go unnoticed and unmanaged. As we've seen from the Big Dig project, the inability to recognize and manage changes to a project can have a devastating impact—in that particular case, to the tune of approximately $11 billion. It's inevitable that changes will occur on a project, so it's imperative that they be managed properly. Measuring and managing change on projects using

25

the SOW are extremely important elements for project success. (This is covered in more detail in Chapter 9.)

Provides a baseline to determine when work has been completed and payment is justified: Again, if the SOW has been written correctly it will identify in "detail" the work that is to be provided to the client. Based on this detailed description, and any approved changes amending the original document, the client and the service provider should have a clear understanding of when work has been completed. When all the products or services have been delivered to and accepted by the client, this will indicate conclusion of the work.

Serves as a determining factor for how profitable the project will be: The more detailed the SOW is in describing the products or services to be delivered, the more detailed and accurate the cost estimate will be. This, however, is only the first step to ensuring the profitability of the engagement. As noted, change is inevitable on projects, and it must be managed properly to ensure project success. If an organization fails to manage changes properly, it could be performing work outside the original scope, which means the work wasn't considered as part of the original budget or price. This type of out-of-scope work will start eating away at the profit margins or the return on investment. If it is managed properly, the out-of-scope work can be considered additional services, which will lead to additional revenues and potentially higher profit margins.

Provides a method of recording, measuring, and analyzing the services and products provided: The SOW provides the project team with a single document that team members can use to specifically address the services and products to be provided to a client under contract. As the primary supporting document to the contract, the SOW establishes the contractual baseline description of each service and product. The team has to reference only this one document to measure and analyze the actual work being performed.

Serves as a necessary baseline for audit purposes: Without an established and agreed-upon baseline document, it becomes impossible to determine whether the work being performed is actually meeting the client's requirements and specifications. It is also impossible to determine when a change occurs on a project. Without a baseline document, any changes made to the project during its lifecycle will not be documented and properly accounted for. Having an SOW in place allows the team to audit the project to determine where changes have occurred from the agreed-upon baseline and to identify the corresponding impact of the changes on the scope, cost, schedule, and manpower. This audit trail of changes provides the organization with the true cost, time, and manpower required to deliver the project. This information is extremely important and beneficial for estimating future projects of similar size and scope.

Protects both the service provider and the client by clearly defining the roles and responsibilities of each party: The SOW captures the roles and responsibilities of both the service provider and the client for the work being performed as part of the project. As such, it reduces the probability of future disputes between the parties regarding who is responsible for the various elements of work being delivered. By clearly defining roles and responsibilities, it allows each party to plan and staff the appropriate resources required to perform the work, thus avoiding potential schedule delays and rework of activities or tasks that may be poorly performed.

Provides a snapshot in time of what the parties agree to: In today's fast-moving, dynamic marketplace, the makeup of the project team is constantly changing. Thus, it's extremely important to have an approved SOW in place that captures the baseline description of the services and products to be delivered at a specific point in time. Having the SOW in place will help avoid potential disputes between the various parties, particularly when there is turnover of the team personnel that made the original agreements. The SOW will legally bind both parties to what their predecessors agreed to. However, it also provides the new members of the team with a baseline document for instituting changes that reflect current needs and requirements.

The benefits of having a detailed SOW on a project are significant and far outweigh the costs associated with developing it. The real-life case studies discussed in this chapter clearly illustrate the negative financial consequences that projects can experience if they do not have an SOW in place. Again, project failures can occur in any industry and any organization at any time. The amount of money lost or wasted on challenged and mismanaged projects can easily reach into the billions of dollars. However, taking the time upfront to develop a detailed SOW and using it to manage the project throughout its lifecycle will help avoid project failures. Doing so will also help projects become more profitable and achieve a higher return on investment for the organization.

NOTES

[1]Michael G. Martin, "Statement of Work: The Foundation for Delivering Successful Service Projects," *PM Network,* Project Management Institute, Inc. (October 1998, Vol. 12, No. 10), pp. 54-57. © 1998, Project Management Institute, Inc.

[2]*Life Application Bible* (co-published by Zondervan Publishing House and Tyndale House Publications, 1991).

[3]Martin, pp. 54–57.

[4]Thomas R. Block, "Project Recovery: Short and Long Term Solutions," *Proceedings of the 29th Annual Project Management Institute 1998 Seminars & Symposium*, Long Beach, CA.

[5]The Standish Group International, "Chaos," Sample Research Paper (West Yarmouth, MA), 1995.

[6]Jim Johnson. 12/99–01/00. "Turning Chaos into Success," *Software Magazine*, Volume 19, Issue 3, 30–32, 34, 39.

[7]Ibid.

[8]The Standish Group International.

[9]Johnson.

[10]Ibid.

[11]Tom Field, "When Bad Things Happen to Good Projects," *CIO*, 15 October 1997.

[12]Ibid.

[13]Tom Ingram, *How To Turn Computer Problems Into Competitive Advantage* (Newtown Square, PA: Project Management Institute, 1998), pp. 82 and 136.

[14]Field, p. 1.

[15]"Watching the Clock," *The Daily Telegraph* (London, UK), 15 April 2000, p. 5.

[16]The Associated Press, "Boston Must Dig Deeper to Pay for 'Big Dig,'" *USA Today,* April 6, 2000, p. 11A.

[17]David H. Maister, *Managing the Professional Service Firm* (New York: Free Press Paperbacks, 1993), p. 71.

[18]Martin, p. 57.

Chapter 3
When to Do an SOW

Let us watch well our beginnings, and results will manage themselves.
—Alexander Clark

There is a great deal of confusion in industry about when an SOW should be required.

If it is developed too early in a project's lifecycle, information needed to develop a detailed description of the work to be performed may not be available. If it's done too late in a project's lifecycle, some of the work may have already been completed or changes may have occurred without being managed properly. This often puts the project manager and the team behind schedule for the rest of the project. The guidance provided in this chapter will help organizations bring order to the chaos that currently exists and establish a consistent approach to determining when an SOW is required.

CONSEQUENCES OF LACK OF GUIDANCE FOR THE PRIVATE SECTOR

The point at which an SOW is developed can vary by industry, as well as by project within an organization. Not knowing when to develop the SOW is often a symptom of the immaturity of an industry's or an organization's project management and contracting skills. This is particularly true in organizations where the development period varies internally among the various lines of business. In these situations, doing an SOW at all is often considered an achievement.

The disparity between organizations regarding when the SOW is developed is illustrated by comparing practices in the public and private sectors. In the public sector, the SOW is considered the most critical document in the acquisition or procurement process. As part of the request for proposal (RFP) or purchase request (PR) process, the SOW has several purposes, including:

- Describing the products or services to be delivered
- Serving as a basis for the contractor's response
- Providing a basis for evaluating proposals
- Defining the roles of the public agency and the contractor
- Providing a point of reference for both the public agency and the contractor to determine when the project has been successfully completed.[1]

As part of the procurement process, planning for the SOW starts as early as possible to ensure that sufficient time is available to draft a quality document. The development may start prior to project authorization to ensure that the SOW is completed and integrated into the procurement package before it is distributed. This approach also helps avoid costly program and project delays later on.

Some government agencies have developed detailed handbooks specific to their organizations. For example, the guidelines for both NASA and DOD require that the SOW be developed as part of the acquisition or procurement process. This is consistent and in accordance with Federal Acquisition Regulation (FAR) guidelines, which require that an SOW be developed as part of the federal contracting process. Agencies like NASA and DOD are on the cutting edge of establishing processes and procedures for developing detailed, quality SOWs in the public sector. Their guidelines should serve as a benchmark for both public and private sector organizations.

When should SOWs be developed in the private sector? The answer to this question is not as clear-cut as it is in the public sector. In the private sector, there is generally a misunderstanding of what an SOW is and how and when it should be used on projects.

One of the reasons for the lack of consensus over when SOW development should occur is because of the way projects originate. In the private sector, most of the work comes from responding to RFPs or from a sales and marketing group generating leads and selling new work. An SOW may or may not be included in the RFP or in the proposal for new work. In most cases, it is not developed as part of the sales process. This practice can then lead to one of the most significant problems facing project managers in the private sector: delivering on unrealistic expectations.

During the sales process, a business developer or sales and marketing group establishes expectations with the client; these expectations are often unrealistic or simply beyond the capabilities of the firm. It's not that these individuals or groups are underhanded, but they often lack the knowledge of what it takes to deliver a project. Moreover, they often either don't know or underestimate the importance of having a detailed SOW developed prior to finalizing the sale or commitments with the client. Unlike in the public sector, no regulations impose the discipline of developing an SOW on a private company.

Historically, the role of the sales and marketing group has been to bring business into the organization and then turn it over to a project manager and implementation team. Sales and marketing groups are generally not concerned with delivery of the project. They tend to have little interest in or incentive to prepare a detailed proposal that ensures that the organization can deliver on what was sold to the client. This lack of foresight and planning within the organization has led to literally billions of dollars being lost every year on failed projects.

The performance measures that drive the sales and delivery teams are different from those driving the project team. The sales and marketing group is measured on the amount of projected revenue from an engagement sold to a client, while the project team is measured on the successful delivery of the project. In one organization I'm familiar with, the sales representatives were paid commission on projected revenues and profitability for engagements sold. The problem with this bonus structure was that the projects weren't always as profitable as they were originally estimated. The sales reps were making a lot of money on unprofitable projects. Once the company realized the problem, the bonus structure was revised. However, the practice of selling engagements without a detailed SOW went unchanged. This meant that projects were still sold on the basis of unrealistic expectations established with the client. If the company had mandated that a detailed SOW be developed as part of the sales process, the estimated revenue and profitability of engagements would have been more accurate, and more projects would have been profitable.

An organization's conflicting performance measures will contribute significantly to the inconsistency of when an SOW is developed. With the sales group focused on trying to close the deal as quickly as possible, the development of a detailed SOW is the last thing on their minds. The delivery team, on the other hand, wants and needs a detailed SOW to ensure that they understand the product or service to be delivered to the client. Without a detailed description, it becomes very difficult for them to be successful. More often than not, the sales team wins this battle. From their perspective, and typically that of executive leadership, it's more important to make the sale and show projected revenue than it is to take the time to develop a detailed document that's not going to help them meet their performance measures. The delivery team must then try to deliver on unrealistic expectations set by the sales group. If organizations are going to improve the likelihood of successfully delivering future projects, it is imperative that the sales and marketing arms of the organization become intimately involved in the development of the SOW and knowledgeable about its importance in the proposal and contract.

> *If the company had mandated that a detailed SOW be developed as part of the sales process, the estimated revenue and profitability of engagements would have been more accurate, and more projects would have been profitable.*

WHEN AN SOW SHOULD BE DONE

In determining when an SOW should be developed, two situations need to be addressed: the competitive bidding situation and the noncompetitive bidding situation. In the private sector, when potential work comes about through an RFP or similar process, this is typically referred to as a *competitive bidding* situation. When a sales or marketing group generates work through direct sales to a client without going through a formal solicitation process, this is referred to as a *noncompetitive bidding* situation.

Competitive Bidding Situations

In almost every case in which an organization in the private sector issues an RFP, that RFP lacks a detailed description of the requirements and specifications of the work to be performed. In rare instances where an organization does have an SOW in place, it is generally at a high level. From the perspective of a service provider, an SOW may not be part of a client's procurement package for many reasons, including:

- Lack of understanding of what an SOW is or why it's needed
- Lack of knowledge about what the problem is or what work needs to be performed
- Lack of knowledge and understanding about how to draft a quality SOW that describes the problem and the work required to provide a solution
- Belief that the description of the work to be performed will be incorporated into the legal terms and conditions
- Insufficient staff and resources to draft an SOW
- Insufficient time allocated to developing the SOW
- Intentionally leaving the scope open-ended to allow the bidders flexibility in their proposals.

Not having a detailed SOW as part of the RFP puts both the client and the service provider at significant risk. The service providers responding to the RFP have no baseline document upon which to base their responses. Without a clear and detailed description of the products and services being requested, there will likely be multiple interpretations of the work to be performed, and consequently multiple solutions proposed.

> *Not having a detailed SOW as part of the RFP puts both the client and the service provider at significant risk.*

The roles and responsibilities of both the client and the service provider will also be unclear. The client will not have a consistent basis upon which to evaluate the various proposals, making it difficult, if not impossible, to select the best solution and provider. Companies tend to have a policy of "ready, fire, aim," wanting immediate or expeditious resolution of their problems without allowing sufficient time for planning. This leads to the implementation of inappropriate "solutions." As a consequence, the initial problem remains unresolved. A vicious cycle known as the "rework cycle" often results, causing the scheduled completion date to be delayed, project costs to increase, and client satisfaction to hit rock bottom.[2]

In a competitive bidding situation, the client should make every effort to develop a detailed SOW as part of the RFP or procurement package. If the client fails to provide a detailed SOW, the service provider should strongly recommend or request it. Another option would be for the service provider to develop a proposal SOW (PSOW) as part of its response.[3] This will provide the client with a detailed description of the work to be performed, as interpreted and understood by the respondent.

If the service provider develops the SOW, it's extremely important that the appropriate personnel be part of the development team. This is particularly true when the sales or marketing function is leading the proposal development. If the individuals responsible for delivering these services are not part of the team, the likelihood that unrealistic expectations will be established with the client increases.

> *If the service provider develops the SOW, it's extremely important that the appropriate personnel be part of the development team.*

Noncompetitive Bidding Situations

In a noncompetitive bidding situation, the client typically does not issue an RFP. The contractor may be a "sole-source" provider of services to the client or a business developer, or a marketing and sales group may have generated the potential work. In these situations, it's almost certain that an SOW has not been developed. The onus is then on the service provider to develop an SOW as soon as possible.[4]

Ideally, the SOW should be developed and agreed upon by both the client and the service provider prior to moving forward with execution of the contract. If the contract is executed with a poorly written SOW, or without an SOW at all, then the service provider should have, at a minimum, an agreed-upon change management process in place with the client. Even with a change management process in place, however, it's going to be difficult (if not impossible) to determine whether a change has occurred.

If you're a project manager taking over a challenged project that doesn't have an SOW in place, your first step should be to meet with the client and request that an SOW be jointly developed immediately. Using this approach to develop the SOW will ensure that both the client and the service provider are in agreement with what work is to be performed under contract. This simple step can turn a challenged project into a success story very quickly.

TYPES OF SOWS AND WHEN THEY APPLY

Two types of SOWs are used in the private sector: the proposal SOW (PSOW) and the contract SOW (CSOW).

Proposal Statement of Work

As the name implies, the PSOW is developed during the sales or proposal process of an engagement. It can be defined as *the SOW developed to support the work being proposed to a client in a noncompetitive bidding situation, as well as the supporting document for the solicitation of work by a client or a contractor to support its response to a solicitation where an SOW was not provided.* Characteristics of the PSOW include:

- First draft or initial SOW
- Based on information provided in the RFP or gathered during the sales process
- Supporting document to the proposal
- May be developed and used by both the client and the service provider
- Used to facilitate development of the bid price.

The PSOW is *not* the proposal to the client. The proposal is a document, prepared by the service provider, that describes the contractor's willingness and capability to provide the requested product or service according to the description and specifications provided in the client's procurement package (e.g., RFP). The proposal is primarily a marketing tool that presents the strengths and capabilities of the organization and is generally not detailed in terms of specifications.

The PSOW, on the other hand, is a supporting document to the proposal that defines in as much detail as possible the product or service to be provided. As noted, an important characteristic of the PSOW is that it can be developed and used by either the client or the service provider. If the client is developing an RFP or procurement package as part of a competitive bidding process, then the PSOW would be included as part of the package. It would clearly define the requirements and specifications of the work the client is seeking. It would also serve as the basis for the contractor's response. In a competitive bidding situation where an SOW is *not* included as part of the procurement package, the service provider may develop a PSOW and submit it to the client as part of its response to the RFP.

This scenario would also apply in a noncompetitive bidding situation, where a proposal has been prepared and submitted to the client without going through a formal solicitation process. The PSOW would clearly identify the work being proposed by the service provider and be included as part of the proposal package submitted to the client. The level of detail of the PSOW is contingent upon the amount of information contained in the RFP or gathered during the sales process. Typically, this information will be at a high level, lacking detailed specifications and requirements. At this stage, the PSOW is more of a functional SOW in that it clearly describes in general terms what work is to be done without providing detailed performance specifications.[5] This is sufficient for simply submitting a proposal; however, it may not be sufficient for supporting the contract.

Contract Statement of Work

In a competitive bidding situation, service providers are often required to respond to RFPs in a very short period of time, ranging anywhere from a couple of days to a couple of weeks. In one case I'm familiar with, a client issued an RFP and requested that responses to the solicitation be provided within two weeks of the issue date. This would be realistic if it were a small project; however, this particular engagement was for the development and deployment of a new IT system worldwide at an approximate cost of $20 million. The short response time didn't allow for the proper planning needed to develop a detailed response or proposal.

For an engagement of this magnitude and complexity, it was simply unrealistic to expect that the information in the response or proposal was accurate enough to execute a contract. In this situation, the potential risk to both the service provider and the client was significant, including a high likelihood of project failure for the service provider.

The PSOW is typically written at a high level and has very few specifics on the work to be performed. For that reason, the PSOW must be taken to the next level and developed into what is known as the contract statement of work (CSOW).

The CSOW is the detailed SOW. It is defined as *the document that identifies the specific requirements and performance measures of the work to be performed, and it supports the contractual terms and conditions of a project.* Characteristics of the CSOW include:

- Supporting document to the contract
- Written factually, based on validated information from performing due diligence
- Technical and schedule requirements stated in terms of desired results
- Defined methods and processes for measuring performance
- Clearly defined deliverables and reporting requirements
- Does not contain marketing, sales, or advertising language.

The CSOW is developed by (1) performing due diligence to determine if the original information in the PSOW is valid, and (2) taking the content in the PSOW to a level of detail sufficient to measure the work to be performed. If a service provider chooses not to do additional due diligence on the engagement and executes the contract based on the PSOW, then there's a high likelihood that the project will be unprofitable to the service provider and unsuccessful in meeting client expectations. If the decision is made to rely on the PSOW instead of developing a CSOW, it becomes critical for the service provider to have a detailed change management process in place.

To illustrate the importance of performing additional due diligence and developing a CSOW, consider the following actual case. A Fortune 100 client issued an RFP for outsourcing all desktop, network, and software support. The RFP identified a certain number of hardware elements that required support; however, one of the service providers responding to the RFP had been doing contract work with the client and knew that the company had more units in its environment than were noted in the RFP. After being selected from the proposal process, the service provider requested that it be allowed to perform additional due diligence on the client's environment to validate the information in the RFP prior to finalizing the contract. The client agreed. In conducting the due diligence, the service provider confirmed that the number in the RFP was underestimated. This led to additional negotiations with the client before the contract was finalized.

By taking this additional step, the service provider was able to estimate accurately the number and types of resources required to perform the work, which also aided in developing a more accurate cost estimate. This in turn helped ensure the profitability of the engagement. By taking the time to do additional due diligence and develop a CSOW, the service provider helped ensure the success and profitability of the project—to the benefit of both parties.

The following guidelines for when to develop an SOW in both competitive and noncompetitive bidding situations will help bring order to the chaos and confusion that currently exist in the private sector, and possibly your own organization, on when an SOW should be developed.

Competitive Bidding Situation
- If an organization is issuing an RFP or procurement package, the SOW should be initiated as early as possible in the process (i.e., as soon as enough information is available to describe the work) by the organization issuing the solicitation, and completed and integrated into the final package distributed to potential vendors.
- If an organization is responding to an RFP or procurement package that does not have an SOW, the first step should be to request that the client provide or develop the document as soon as possible. If the client is unable or unwilling to develop an SOW, then a proposal SOW (PSOW) should be developed as part of the response to the RFP. Upon finalizing the negotiations of the contract, a contract SOW (CSOW) should be developed.

Noncompetitive Bidding Situation
- If an organization has submitted a proposal to the client without going through a formal solicitation process, then a PSOW should be developed and made part of the proposal package.
- If the proposal and PSOW are accepted by the client, the service provider should then perform additional due diligence and develop a CSOW prior to finalizing the contract.

- If a contract is executed without an SOW as part of the agreement, then the client and the service provider should jointly develop a CSOW as soon as possible. Once the CSOW has been approved, it should be attached as a supporting document to the contract.
- In a noncompetitive situation, some work may have already been completed prior to the execution of a contract. In this situation, the client and the service provider should jointly develop a CSOW and execute a contract as soon as possible. The CSOW in this case should be specific to any remaining work to be performed on the project.
- If taking over a challenged project that has a contract but not an SOW (or has one that is poorly written), the service provider should meet with the client and jointly develop a new CSOW or revise the existing one for all remaining work. Again, the document should be drafted as expeditiously as possible and attached to the contract.

NOTES

[1] NASA Handbook 5600.2A—*Statements of Work Handbook,* 23 July 1993, p. 6.

[2] "The $2000 Hour: How Managers Influence Project Performance Through the Rework," *Project Management Journal,* Volume XXV, March 1994.

[3] Harold Kerzner, Ph.D., *Project Management: A Systems Approach to Planning, Scheduling, and Controlling*, 5th ed. (New York: Van Nostrand Reinhold, 1995), p. 583.

[4] Ibid.

[5] Peter S. Cole, *How to Write a Statement of Work* (Vienna, VA: Management Concepts, Inc., 1999), pp. 2–11.

Chapter 4

Who Should Develop the SOW

*In the end, the wisdom of teams is within the team itself. It is not in creating
the high-performance organization, managing transformational change,
enforcing corporate performance ethics, or inspiring new dimensions of leadership. It is in a small group of people so committed to something larger than
themselves that they will not be denied.*
— *Jon R. Katzenbach and Douglas K. Smith*
The Wisdom of Teams: Creating the High-Performance Organization
(New York: HarperBusiness, 1994), p. 259.

Service providers in today's marketplace are under intense pressure to deliver products and services to their clients more quickly
and efficiently than ever before. This pressure arises in part
from the intense competition among organizations wanting to be first
to market with a new product or service and to be recognized as "best
in class" within their industry. To respond effectively to these increasing demands, service providers must have a specialized workforce that
is highly trained and can adapt to changes quickly.[1] Having the correct resources assigned to an activity or project is critical to ensuring
that it is completed successfully.

The saying, "a chain is only as strong as its weakest link," applies to
the team responsible for developing the SOW. The quality of the document will be only as good as the individual team members responsible
for developing it. If the correct skills and resources aren't assigned to
the effort, certain areas of the SOW will be more susceptible to risk.
These areas of risk will be the weak links in the SOW that will ultimately lead to project failure.

This chapter focuses on who should be responsible for developing the SOW to ensure that it is of the highest quality possible. It also addresses how to build cohesiveness among the team members to ensure that they have a common vision and understanding of the project.

BUILDING THE TIGER TEAM

One of the most important, and sometimes most difficult, steps in developing an SOW is identifying and acquiring the appropriate resources to be part of the development team. The best way to determine the appropriate resources is to first develop a work breakdown structure for the project (covered in detail in Chapter 5.) The WBS is a decomposition of the products or services to be provided to the client down to the lowest manageable level possible. Once the WBS has been developed, the project manager or proposal manager can identify the skills and resources required to perform the various tasks.

When a team has a common objective and each team member is laser-focused on that objective, the potential for project success is unlimited.

A representative from each of the functional groups responsible for a portion of the project is then asked to participate in development of the SOW. Having representation from each of these groups helps ensure that the expectations established in the SOW are realistic and achievable.

This scenario sounds simple and straightforward. Unfortunately, real life doesn't always play out sensibly, particularly when it comes to developing SOWs. As noted in Chapter 3, one of the most significant problems facing service providers in the private sector today is the lack of a detailed SOW during the sales or proposal process. Ideally, a team of subject matter experts (SMEs) would be working together on the SOW during this phase of the project to ensure that the firm can actually deliver what is being sold to the client. However, in most cases the SOW doesn't even exist during this phase of the project; in those rare cases where it does exist, it tends to be at a very high level and lack sufficient detail.

Most service providers today continue to use traditional project management processes and techniques for implementing and managing projects, as well as for developing SOWs. This traditional approach is characterized by sequential, task-oriented thinking. Each functional group within the organization tends to focus on its area of specialty, with little or no regard to the other functional areas. When one team is finished with its portion of the work, it passes it on to the next team.

This "professional services assembly line" approach is typically found in organizations that have a separate sales and marketing function. The sales team is generally responsible for identifying new opportunities and generating revenue for the firm—and is less concerned with how the project will actually be delivered.

To illustrate this sequential type of approach, let's take a look at a sample IT outsourcing project. We'll assume that the lifecycle for this project consists of six phases: marketing, assessment, planning and design, implementation, operation and maintenance, and closeout (see Figure 4-1).[2] The project is initiated by the sales or marketing team responding to an RFP from the client. Once the proposal has been accepted and the contract signed, the sales team turns its focus toward generating additional business from the client or from new opportunities identified elsewhere. After the planning and design have been completed, implementation of the product or service can be initiated. Implementation is the responsibility of the service integration or implementation team. Once implementation has been completed, the project is turned over to a group that we'll call the steady-state delivery team. This team remains with the project throughout the contract period or until the contract is terminated.

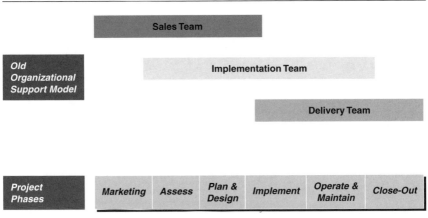

Figure 4-1. Sequential Delivery Approach

This traditional approach offers certain benefits: (1) it provides a structured methodology for delivering the product or service sold to the client; (2) it allows the functional groups to focus on their area of specialty; (3) it allows the service provider to respond very quickly to a client in a competitive bidding situation; and (4) it's better than not having any approach at all.[3] However, the costs of this type of assembly line approach far outweigh the benefits to the firm.

Even though this approach may allow the service provider to respond expeditiously in a competitive bidding situation, the response generally does not incorporate input from the SMEs responsible for delivering the project. Misperceptions and miscommunications about the scope of the project and the roles and responsibilities of the various functional groups can result. Faster, in this case, is not necessarily better. The expediency of the response doesn't allow sufficient time to accurately document the clients' requirements and specifications for the project. This, in turn, leads to poorly written SOWs and, ultimately, project failure.

With the extreme pressure being applied to service providers to respond and deliver products and services faster than ever before, a sequential approach is not the best methodology to follow in developing the SOW. Service providers often find that they're well into the implementation phase of a project before they realize that the commitments made during the sales process were unrealistic and unachievable. The challenge to organizations then is determining what approach should be used to ensure that the appropriate resources are identified and that they participate in the development of the SOW.

Determining the right approach is even more challenging when dealing with a well-established organization that is sales-driven and where the functional boundaries and lines of authority are firmly established. One approach to breaking down these boundaries and improving communication and teamwork among the functional disciplines is the application of concurrent engineering (CE) methodologies.[4] The basic premise behind this approach is doing tasks in parallel rather than sequentially. Joseph Cleetus of West Virginia University's Concurrent Engineering Research Center defines concurrent engineering as "a systematic approach to the integrated development of a product and its related processes—from conception to disposal—that emphasizes response to customer expectations and embodies team values of cooperation, trust, and sharing in such a manner that decision making proceeds with large intervals of parallel working by all life-cycle perspectives, synchronized by comparatively brief exchanges to produce consensus."[5,6]

"Concurrent engineering was conceived as a method of improving productivity and responsiveness in manufacturing operations. Eastman Kodak pioneered the process as a response to a new product introduction by one of its competitors, Fuji. To respond quickly to Fuji's introduction of the disposable camera, Kodak reengineered its development process to speed introduction of Kodak's version of the disposable camera to market. Rather than develop the product sequentially, Kodak brought product designers, manufacturing engineers, and other members of the development effort together to work as an integrated team."[7] By using this CE approach, the team was able to reduce the development process by half. The stunning results of this project gave rise to the popularity of CE methods, which have since been embraced by the automotive and aerospace industries.[8,9]

The competitive edge gained by using CE is that it helps the service provider develop a detailed, quality SOW for the project. By having SMEs participate in the development of this foundational document at the beginning of the project, the service provider is able to deliver services more expeditiously and at a lower cost while still meeting the client's expectations. The CE approach doesn't eliminate functional barriers, but rather integrates them into a cohesive team, which has a common goal and is focused on delivering the project on time, within budget, and in accordance with the clients' requirements. By integrating the functional SMEs into one team, they are able to respond immediately to changes that occur on the project, rather than having to go through a sequential or hierarchical escalation process. This added flexibility helps ensure that changes are addressed expeditiously and by the appropriate resources.[10]

This integrated project team is referred to as the "TIGER" team: Totally Integrated Groups of Expert Resources.

What does this integrated, cohesive project team look like? The team comprises SMEs from each of the functional disciplines responsible for a portion of the project, along with a project manager who acts as the team lead. This integrated concept allows the SMEs to pool their knowledge of requirements, processes and procedures, as-

> *The one member who is critical to the success of the team and project, and must be on every TIGER team, is the client representative.*

sumptions, constraints, and solutions to ensure that this knowledge is captured and documented appropriately within the SOW.

This integrated project team is referred to as the "TIGER" team: <u>T</u>otally <u>I</u>ntegrated <u>G</u>roups of <u>E</u>xpert <u>R</u>esources. A sample TIGER team for the IT outsourcing project discussed earlier may include a project manager, account (sales) manager, help desk SME, network SME, process consultant, reporting SME, acquisition SME, asset management SME, and the client (see Figure 4-2).[11,12] Every member of the TIGER team has an important role to play in ensuring the successful completion of the project. However, the one member who is critical to the success of the team and project, and must be on every TIGER team, is the client representative. Without the client's participation, input, and support, the likelihood of accurately capturing and meeting their needs and expectations is greatly decreased.

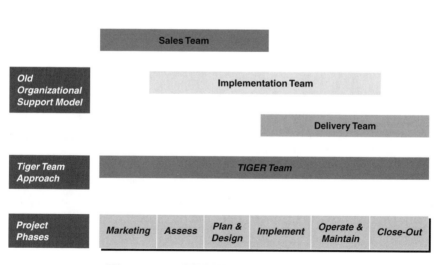

Figure 4-2. TIGER Team Approach

Implementation Strategies

Implementation of a TIGER team approach for developing SOWs may require fundamental changes to an organization's overall structure. Specifically, it may require reorganization into a hierarchy of teams or a matrix organization. Top management support is crucial to the successful implementation of any changes to the organizational structure.

Before the TIGER team approach can be implemented, several criteria must be met. First, the organization must have a proven methodology for executing projects. If it does not, a methodology for determining the proper order of work to be performed should be designed or adopted. This includes determining the predecessor and successor relationships between the various steps or phases of the project lifecycle. Second, once the sequential steps have been captured, the organization can then determine which elements can be performed simultaneously or in parallel.[13] Third, the roles and responsibilities of each of the TIGER team members must be clearly defined and understood by the entire team.[14] This will improve the coordination and communication of the team members, which in turn will reduce the duplication of effort.

Implementation of this new team-based structure may be a major change effort for the organization. "Two aspects must be addressed to create this readiness for change: discrepancy and efficacy. *Discrepancy* is about demonstrating that there is a problem that needs to be addressed. Publicizing weak profit margins or marginal customer service critiques can create a sense of discrepancy."[15] The second aspect is *efficacy*, that is: "'How do we improve this situation?' It must be shown that the TIGER team will create better outcomes for the firm."[16] Once the organization realizes that the status quo is no longer sufficient and it sees an effective strategy for improving the quality of its SOWs and its operations, readiness for the change effort will have been created.[17,18]

Once a change-readiness effort has been undertaken and the TIGER team concept is ready for implementation throughout the organization, one additional issue will have to be addressed. Integrated teams can be very resource-intensive, particularly in industry sectors that have chronic labor shortfalls. Accordingly, a TIGER team may not be suitable for managing the entire lifecycle of smaller projects.[19,20] The decision to use this approach is strictly a management call. However, it is strongly recommended that the TIGER team be used for developing the SOW for every project, regardless of size or industry. This will help ensure that the SOW accurately captures the requirements and specifications identified by the client and that the firm can actually deliver to those expectations.

Benefits of the TIGER Team Approach

The TIGER team concept can be applied to any industry or organization that is performing projects. In addition to flexibility, applying a TIGER team strategy within an organization offers many benefits:

- "Services will more frequently meet the customer's requirements and specifications
- Achievable service levels will be established in the SOW
- Customer satisfaction will increase
- Teamwork and partnering with the client will be improved
- Cycle time for implementing services will decrease
- Probability of reactivating or reinitiating the project at a later date will be reduced
- Revenue and profit margins will increase
- Probability of project failure will be reduced
- Employee retention will be improved
- Flexibility to respond quickly to changes in the customer requirements will be improved."[21,22]

Implementing the TIGER team approach will drastically improve the quality of the SOWs developed. It will also systematically improve client satisfaction, employee morale, and the success of future projects.

TIGER Team Considerations

Implementing the TIGER team approach is critical to the development of quality SOWs for an organization. If the correct resources aren't identified and acquired for the team, then the quality of the SOW will be in question, as will the future of the project on which it is based. Important considerations in implementing and applying the TIGER team approach include:

1. Develop a detailed WBS to determine the appropriate resources.

The first step in accurately identifying the appropriate resources required to assist in the development of an SOW is to develop a detailed WBS. In a competitive bidding situation, this may be difficult to do if the response time is short. However, without decomposing the project down to the smallest manageable level possible, it is difficult to determine the skills and resources required to deliver it successfully. If the response time is short, the WBS should be as detailed as possible based on the information available.

2. Keep the team small, but fully represented.

To keep the TIGER team effective, it should be kept as small as possible, with the minimum number of representatives from the various functional areas. However, every functional discipline responsible for a portion of the project should be represented on the team. Excluding any discipline that has responsibility for the project creates a potential risk to the quality of the document. To ensure proper representation throughout the development of the SOW (as well as the rest of the project), each functional discipline should identify a primary and secondary representative to the team. If the primary representative is unable to participate, then the secondary representative should fill in to maintain continuity.

3. Select SMEs who are team players and have approval authority.

The primary and secondary representatives from the functional disciplines should be recognized subject matter experts within their particular areas of expertise. It is critical that these representatives have approval authority for agreeing to and signing off on the requirements and specifications documented in the SOW. If they do not, the development process could be delayed to the point that the project fails. The TIGER team is an integrated team whose success is dependent on the cohesiveness of the individual representatives. Therefore, it is important that each of the representatives be a consummate team player willing to work in an integrated team environment.

The project manager does not have to be the SME for the project. The PM's role on the TIGER team is to facilitate and coordinate the SMEs from the supporting functional disciplines. The PM has overall responsibility and accountability for ensuring that the SOW is completed to the highest level of quality possible and is approved by all the necessary entities.

4. Collocate team members.

If at all possible, the team members should all be located together during the development of the SOW. The coordination and communication needed to ensure that all aspects of the project are being captured and documented is best done through collocation. It will also help minimize duplication of effort across the functional disciplines.

Unfortunately, collocation is not always feasible. In situations where a virtual team is necessary, it is important that face-to-face meetings be held as often as possible to ensure that team continuity and structure are maintained. When working virtually, communication with the team members is essential to keep the team focused on the work at hand, as well as to maintain intangible links with the other team members.[23,24]

5. Maintain consistent and frequent communications.

Communication is critical to the success of the TIGER team approach. Without consistent and frequent communications among the various team members, certain elements of the project may not be captured, or duplication of effort may occur. The project manager has primary responsibility for ensuring that communication is conducted appropriately and accurately throughout the process. As noted, this is particularly important when the development team cannot be collocated.

If team members feel like information is being withheld from them or that they're not privy to issues related to the process, they may retaliate. If this happens, the quality of the SOW, as well as the project, is at risk.

BUILDING THE CONE OF COHESION

Forming and implementing a TIGER team approach is only the first step in ensuring that the SOW development team is successful. You may be fortunate enough to have the best resources in the organization working on this effort; however, if each member has different objectives or perceptions about what the project should be accomplishing, then there will be problems. "Have you ever witnessed a sporting event where two teams were involved in competition and somehow the underdog miraculously defeats the overwhelming favorite? There are often many debates following the event as to how the team with the best players could lose to a team who shouldn't even be on the same playing field. For whatever reason, though, not only were they on the same playing field, but they played to a level equal to or above that of the superior team and WON."[25]

Many attribute this phenomenon to karma or momentum, or just plain luck. During my athletic career I had the fortune (or misfortune) to be on both types of teams.[26] When you're on the team that the newspapers have picked to walk away with the championship and you fall short of the goal, it's one of the worst feelings in the world. However, when you're the underdog and you defeat Goliath, it's one of the best feelings in the world. What makes a team perform at a level above their perceived skill level?

The common denominator I've observed both as a spectator and as a player is that the winning team plays as a cohesive unit with a common goal. Without a common goal, the individual players lose focus of what they're trying to achieve. This type of situation also occurs in business and industry every day. If a team is assembled for a specific project, yet the main goal or objective of the initiative is not made known to them, they will determine their own individual objective for the project. If the objectives of the project are made clear to each of the team members, the chance of delivering the project successfully is greatly increased. To illustrate this, I developed Martin's Cone of Team Cohesion (see Figure 4-3).[27]

> *If the objectives of the project are made clear to each of the team members, the chance of delivering the project successfully is greatly increased.*

At the initiation of the project, the objectives are not clearly defined, and each team member is doing his or her own thing. At this stage, the team is often in chaos. As the objectives of the project become more clearly defined and understood, the team starts to gel and come together as a cohesive unit. When a team has a common objective and each team member becomes laser-focused on that objective, their potential to succeed is unlimited.

Just as the underdog in the sporting event is able to overcome a team perceived as being superior, so it is with project teams in industry. You may have two teams within your organization working on similar projects; one team may be performing well, while the other is not performing up to the organization's expectations. The team that is performing well likely understands its objectives and what it takes to accomplish its goal.

The project manager plays a critical role in ensuring that the team clearly understands the objectives to be accomplished and that each individual understands his or her role and responsibilities on the project. Without the leadership of a central figure (i.e., the project

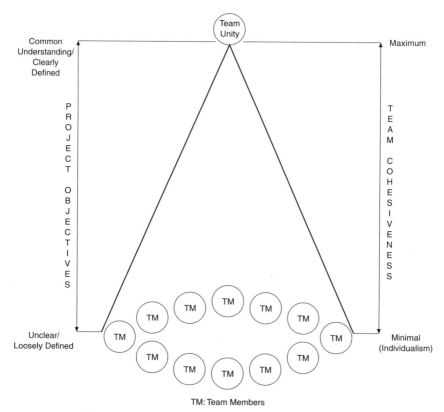

Figure 4-3. Martin's Cone of Team Cohesion

manager) to identify the project objectives, each individual member of the team will develop his or her own objectives.

Another problem comes into play when an organization measures the performance of its employees by pre-established objectives (i.e., management by objectives, or MBOs). If the individual team members are recruited from the various functional disciplines, more than likely each of them will have inconsistent MBOs. This situation can easily be corrected by moving to a strong matrix or TIGER team structure where the importance and focus are placed on the project. In this type of structure, each team member will have the same objective (e.g., successfully deliver Project X within the schedule and budget established).

If TIGER teams are to reach a level of excellence, they first need to ensure that they have a common goal and objectives and that each member of the team understands these without exception. There is a direct correlation between the cohesion of the team and the quality of the SOW developed. If cohesion is achieved, then the quality of the SOW will be high. These, in turn, will more than likely correlate to

> *There is a direct correlation between the cohesion of the team and the quality of the SOW developed.*

the project being successful. Excellence can then be achieved in developing SOWs and delivering successful projects for the organization.

Implementation of a TIGER team or similar team structure is critical to the development of a quality SOW and ultimately the success of the project. Organizations in today's business environment are facing intense competition, not only on the local and national levels, but also globally. The intensity of this competition is pressuring organizations to deliver quality products and services more expeditiously and efficiently than ever before.

This pressure to expedite and deliver at the lowest cost possible often causes organizations to make poor decisions. These include not taking sufficient time to plan the project and assign the appropriate resources to develop a detailed SOW. When an organization starts taking these types of shortcuts, it's just a matter of time before projects fail.

To meet increasing market demands, it is imperative that a highly trained and specialized team of subject matter experts be assigned to the project from the initiation of planning through its completion. For this team to be successful, it is also critical that the client be represented on the team to ensure that its requirements and expectations are being met. This client involvement will also decrease the likelihood of scope creep and rework on the project. Establishing this type of team structure will significantly increase an organization's ability to achieve project excellence and deliver quality products and services in the most expeditious and efficient manner possible.

NOTES

[1]Leyland F. Pitt, Richard T. Watson, and C. Bruce Kavan, 1995. "Service Quality: A Measure of Information Systems Effectiveness," *MIS Quarterly,* 19: 173–187.

[2]Michael G. Martin, Michael R. Weeks, and Kevin J. Davis, "Delivering Successful Service and Outsourcing Projects Using Concurrent Engineering Methodologies," *Proceedings of the 29th Annual Seminars & Symposium*, Long Beach, CA (1998). Project Management Institute, Inc. All rights reserved.

[3]Ibid., p. 2.

[4]Ibid., p.1.

[5]Ibid.

[6]Concurrent Engineering Research Center (CERC) Homepage. 1998 Overview: Concurrent Engineering (February 3). http://www.cerc.wvu.edu/overview.html.

[7]Martin, Weeks, and Davis, p. 1.

[8]James Hammer and James Champy, *Reengineering the Corporation* (New York: HarperBusiness, 1993).

[9]Dorothy, H. Leonard-Barton, Kent Bowen, Kim B. Clark, Charles A. Holloway, and Steven C. Wheelwright. 1994. "How to Integrate Work and Deepen Expertise." *Harvard Business Review* 72, no. 5: 121–30.

[10]Martin, Weeks, and Davis, p. 3.

[11]Ibid.

[12]Michael G. Martin, Michael R. Weeks, and Kevin J. Davis. 1998. "TIGER Teams on Outsourcing Projects: They're Grreat!" *PM Network*, pp. 50–53.

[13]Michael G. Martin, Michael R. Weeks, and Kevin J. Davis, "Delivering Successful Service and Outsourcing Projects Using Concurrent Engineering Methodologies," *Proceedings of the 29th Annual Seminars & Symposium*, Long Beach, CA (1998). Project Management Institute, Inc. All rights reserved.

[14]"Getting It Done," *Fast Company*, June 2000, p. 150.

[15]Michael G. Martin, Michael R. Weeks, and Kevin J. Davis, "Delivering Successful Service and Outsourcing Projects Using Concurrent Engineering Methodologies," *Proceedings of the 29th Annual Seminars & Symposium*, Long Beach, CA (1998). Project Management Institute, Inc. All rights reserved.

[16]Ibid.

[17]Achilles A. Armenakis, Stanley G. Harris, and Kevin W. Mossholder. 1993. Creating Readiness for Organizational Change. *Human Relations* 46: 681–703.

[18]Michael G. Martin, Michael R. Weeks, and Kevin J. Davis. 1998. "TIGER Teams on Outsourcing Projects: They're Grreat!" *PM Network*, p. 52.

[19]Ibid.

[20]Michael G. Martin, Michael R. Weeks, and Kevin J. Davis, "Delivering Successful Service and Outsourcing Projects Using Concurrent Engineering Methodologies," *Proceedings of the 29th Annual Seminars & Symposium*, Long Beach, CA (1998). Project Management Institute, Inc. All rights reserved.

[21]Ibid.

[22]Michael G. Martin, Michael R. Weeks, and Kevin J. Davis. 1998. "TIGER Teams on Outsourcing Projects: They're Grreat!" *PM Network*, p. 53.

[23]Jaclyn Kostner. *Knights of the Tele-Round Table* (New York: Warner Books, 1994).

[24]Clinton A Jullens. 1997. "Life on *Venture Star*™: The Use of Integrated Product Teams to Perform Concurrent Engineering on a 21st Century Space Program," *Proceedings of the 28th Annual Project Management Institute 1997 Seminars & Symposium*, Chicago, IL, pp. 12–18.

[25]Mike Martin. "Understanding Team Cohesion For Building High-Performance Teams." *Successful Project Management* (Vienna, VA: Management Concepts, Inc., November 1999). pp. 2–3.

[26]Ibid.

[27]Ibid., p. 2.

Part 2

Building the Statement of Work

We have explored *what* the SOW is, *why* it's needed, *when* it should be done, and *who* should develop it. Understanding the answers to these basic questions is critical not only to the development of a quality SOW, but also to the success of the project. Without this basic knowledge and understanding, both the SOW and the project will be at serious risk.

We will now take the process to the next level: development of an SOW. The next three chapters will cover what I refer to as the F3 methodology. This methodology consists of three phases: *Foundation*, *Framing*, and *Finalizing* the SOW. The *foundation* phase involves laying the foundation for the development of the document. During this phase, as much information as possible is gathered about the project and the client. This phase is critical to the quality of the SOW. If little information is available or if the information gathered is not accurate, then it will negatively impact the quality of the document. However, if the information is detailed and accurate, a quality document can be developed.

The *framing* phase addresses how the SOW should be structured or customized for a particular client or engagement. The structure and type of content to be included in the document will also be identified during this phase.

Last but not least is *finalizing* the SOW. During this phase, negotiations are conducted between the client and the service provider to address any outstanding issues that require resolution prior to finalizing the SOW. The negotiations may require that revisions be made to the document. Any proposed revisions must be agreed to by both the client and the service provider. Once revisions have been approved and the appropriate changes made, then the document can be finalized and included as an attachment to the legal contract. At this point, the document is considered the contract SOW.

The F3 methodology may sound familiar to you. If you have ever been through the experience of building a home, you can see that the process for developing an SOW is very similar. For example, the first thing you would do in constructing a home is to form the foundation for the structure. If the foundation is not constructed properly, then the structure placed upon it will be at risk of failing; thus, it's important that the foundation be solid and structurally sound. The next step is to frame the house for the walls and roof. The framing can be customized based on any special requirements you may have. Once the framing has been completed, the structure is formed or finalized, the contract is signed, and you take ownership.

Chapter 5

Building the SOW Foundation

Nothing is particularly hard if you divide it into small jobs.

—*Henry Ford*

The first phase of the F3 methodology is building the *foundation* of the SOW. This phase consists of two parts: performing a due diligence analysis and developing a work breakdown structure (WBS). The due diligence analysis is a detailed investigation or analysis of the client's requirements and specifications to determine the true scope of the product or service being proposed or sold to the client. This step is extremely important in both the competitive and the noncompetitive bidding process, and it may be repeated throughout the development of both the PSOW and the CSOW. The detail of this analysis correlates directly with the detail of the next element, which is the development of the WBS. The WBS is a decomposition of the product or service being provided to the client. The detail of the WBS plays a critical role in determining the quality of the SOW.

As with building a house, it is critical that the foundation of the project (i.e., the SOW) be firmly established. The elements covered in this chapter will help ensure that the foundation of the SOW is structurally sound and will adequately support the delivery of the final product or service to the client.

PERFORMING DUE DILIGENCE

> *Due Diligence*: *Such inquiry as a diligent man, intent upon ascertaining a fact, would ordinarily make, and it is inquiry made with diligence and good faith to ascertain the truth, and must be an inquiry as full as the circumstances of the situation will permit.*
> —Black's Law Dictionary, 5th Edition.

Performing due diligence is the most frequently overlooked step in the SOW development process. This is particularly true in competitive bidding situations where an RFP is issued. Often there is simply not enough time to perform a proper analysis of the RFP to determine the validity and accuracy of the information it contains. Unless the service provider has previous knowledge or experience with the client, an assumption may have to be made that the information is valid and accurate. However, special care should be taken when responding to an RFP where the data appear to be inaccurate or when the client is requesting a very quick turnaround for responses.

I'm familiar with organizations that have issued RFPs that were so vague and contained such little information that it was impossible to develop an accurate proposal response. This problem is not limited to a particular industry or organization. In fact, it can occur just as easily in a Fortune 100 company as in a brand new start-up. The misinformation in the RFP can be attributed to: (1) lack of client knowledge on how to draft a detailed RFP, and (2) a perception by the client that the service provider is an expert on the particular product or service that's being requested, so they should not need a lot of information or time to respond to a request. Service providers are guilty as well. They often encourage the client's reliance on their "expertise," telling clients that they can deliver on any project without taking time to plan and document the scope of the work to be performed. In this scenario, no one wins.

In today's competitive marketplace, some organizations or individuals may find it inconceivable to allocate any amount of time to planning, particularly as part of the proposal process. The assumption is that if a product or service needs to be implemented quickly, then the RFP should be issued and the contract awarded as expeditiously as possible. Responding solely to this need for immediacy does not allow sufficient time for the planning that needs to occur. If anything is missed during the proposal process, then the assumption is that it will be addressed during the implementation phase. In other words, the thinking is that the project will be changing, so why take the time to do any type of detailed planning up front?

Organizations rationalize this thinking and then reinforce it with the inertia created by the "business-as-usual" approach: We've always done our projects this way, so why change? This thought process occurs even though overwhelming evidence shows that doing projects this way ultimately leads to failed projects and costs the organization millions, and possibly billions, of dollars. The saying "there's never enough time to do something right, but there's always time to do it over," applies here. It's this type of thinking and approach in competitive bidding situations that leads not only to project failures, but also could ultimately lead to the failure of the organization.

The need for due diligence is not limited to competitive bidding situations. In some respects, it is even more important in a noncompetitive bidding situation, where a sales or marketing group is generating new business opportunities with a new or existing client. As noted, if this group's performance measures are based on bringing revenue into the firm, then they may end up selling a product or service that will not adequately solve the client's problem or meet the client's expectations. To mitigate against this, it is important that due diligence be conducted on the client's organization as well as on the issue that has created the need for the project.

> *Unless some level of due diligence is conducted, the outcome will be the same: setting up unrealistic expectations that can't possibly be met. This, in turn, leads to a dissatisfied client and an unprofitable project for the service provider.*

It often seems to be easier simply to make an unsolicited proposal to a client without truly knowing anything about the client or its needs. As in the competitive bidding situation, this rush to sign a contract can have serious consequences. Unless some level of due diligence is conducted, the outcome will be the same: setting up unrealistic expectations that can't possibly be met. This, in turn, leads to a dissatisfied client and an unprofitable project for the service provider.

Five-Step Process for Performing Due Diligence

There are different ways to perform due diligence, ranging from simple to complex, and taking anywhere from a couple of days to a couple of months. These variations are contingent upon the type of project or information being gathered and analyzed. For example, the due diligence performed for the construction of a nuclear power facility will be larger in scope and require more resources than that performed for the construction of a new house. Although a due diligence process is performed in both cases, the level of detail will vary greatly.

It is important that the service provider implement and consistently follow a standard process for performing due diligence. I recommend a five-step process that can be used for any industry or project (see Figure 5-1).

Step 1: Define the Scope and Purpose

Prior to beginning the due diligence analysis, the scope and purpose must be clearly defined. The purpose statement should provide justification for performing the analysis. If sufficient justification is not provided, then it's possible that an analysis is not warranted and should be reconsidered. Situations that justify performing a detailed analysis include:

- Lack of detailed information in the RFP.
- Questionable validity and accuracy of data.
- Insufficient time allowed for proper planning in responding to an RFP. (In this situation, the due diligence analysis should be performed after the proposal has been accepted, but prior to development of the CSOW.)
- Request by the client to perform a due diligence analysis.
- Little known about a prospective client, the client's environment, and/or the proposed project.

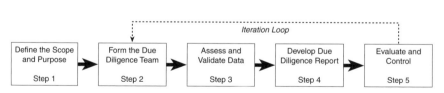

Figure 5-1. Five-Step Due Diligence Process

Once the purpose has been documented and justified, the next is to define the scope of the analysis. The due diligence effort often does not have a well-defined scope statement. This can be attributed to the nature of the project, which is basically an investigation of an unknown or a validation or assessment of data that are perceived to be factual. This lack of knowledge of what should be analyzed leads to a poor scope statement of the work to be performed. Without a proper scope statement, it becomes very easy for the due diligence team to analyze data or to investigate areas outside of the scope of the project being proposed. This could potentially increase the total estimated cost as well as delay completion of the analysis.

One method for ensuring that a proper scope statement is in place is to develop a WBS of the analysis to be conducted. This will help clearly define and communicate the boundaries of the analysis to be performed. At this phase of the project, it is unlikely that a project manager has been assigned; thus, development of the WBS will likely fall to a sales or proposal manager. As part of this process, the manager will identify and prioritize the data that need to be gathered and analyzed. Once the WBS has been completed, the sales or proposal manager can determine the skills and resources required to perform the tasks identified.

Step 2: Forming the Due Diligence Team

As with any project, it is extremely important that the correct skills and resources be identified and acquired to perform the due diligence analysis. Ideally, the due diligence team should consist of subject matter experts (SMEs) for the areas being analyzed. This, in essence, is the genesis of the TIGER team (discussed in Chapter 4). Due to the uniqueness of each analysis, it is not practical to identify a generic team or organizational structure. However, there is one functional role that is consistently required on every analysis—project manager.

This responsibility may naturally fall to the sales or proposal manager. Ideally, however, a project manager is assigned to the project at this point and remains with the project throughout its lifecycle. This individual will be responsible for coordinating and facilitating the team during the due diligence analysis. Responsibilities will also include developing a detailed project plan, which will include a communications plan, issue management plan, risk management plan, change management plan, WBS, and schedule. If a project manager is not

ative, then there's a good chance that the analysis
ted on time and within the established budget.
ividual manage the overall analysis will help en-
duplication of effort and that the team members
cope of the initiative.

he discussion on TIGER teams, it's just as impor-
tant during the due diligence analysis as it is in delivering the project
to have SMEs participate in analyzing the data specific to their area of
specialty. Having SMEs perform the due diligence analysis significantly decreases the chance of overlooking a critical data element in
the SOW. This, in turn, increases the likelihood that a quality SOW
will be developed and the project will be successful. Once the required
resources have been identified, the roles and responsibilities of the
individual team members can be defined. Mapping these roles and
responsibilities to the due diligence tasks identified in the WBS will
create a responsibility assignment matrix (RAM) for the effort.

Assigning responsibilities to the individual team members can be
illustrated by several different methods. The most common are:

RACI
- **R**esponsible for Doing
- **A**pprove
- **C**ontributes/Consults
- **I**nformed

PARIS
- **P**articipates in Doing
- **A**pprove
- **R**esponsible for Doing
- **I**nformed
- **S**ign-off

Adopting these simple methods is extremely beneficial in identifying who is responsible for doing the work, who can approve it, who
contributes to or is consulted on the work, and who is simply informed
of the project status. Taking the time to identify the individual responsibilities will greatly reduce the likelihood that work will be du-
plicated and gaps overlooked. A sample RAM, using the **RACI** method,
is shown in Figure 5-2.

Due Diligence Analysis	Project Manager	Service Line SMA	Analyst	Sponsor
Develop WBS	R	C	C	I
Develop Analysis Process	A	R	C	I
Assess Data	A	R	C	I
Validate Data	A	R	C	I
Analyze Data	A	C	R	I
Prepare Report and Recommendations	R	C	C	A

Legend

R - Responsible
A - Approve
C - Contribute/Consult
I - Informed

Figure 5-2. Responsibility Assignment Matrix (RAM)

Once the responsibilities have been assigned, the team will then be ready to move forward to Step 3.

Step 3: Assessing and Validating Data

Once the scope has been defined and the resources identified, the next step is to begin assessing and validating the data on the project. The data may be taken from an RFP that has been issued (competitive bidding situation), or it can be data that are gathered as part of the sales process (noncompetitive bidding situation). For the purpose of this discussion, the term *data* refers to both the quantitative and the qualitative information to be analyzed. The quantitative data can be elements such as the number of desktops and servers to be supported, the number of screens to be developed for a web site, or the number and types of doors to be installed in a home. Qualitative data will include processes and procedures that may be required as part of the project. For example, if a client issues an RFP for upgrading its on-site help desk, the client might include the process by which the calls are currently being managed as well as the established service levels.

The service provider will need to assess and verify that the process and service levels are factual, documenting any discrepancies.

The first step in assessing and validating data is for the due diligence team, working with the client if possible, to develop a process overview. This overview should address how to identify and analyze the critical data for the engagement.

Including the client in the development process can help ensure buy-in and acceptance. However, service providers tend to be reluctant about including the client in any type of analysis. The perception is that if they ask the client to participate, it may be perceived that they're not subject matter experts and they lack sufficient knowledge to deliver the project successfully. The client may perpetuate this reasoning by telling the service provider that they're paying them a lot of money to do this work, so why should they provide resources to assist in this effort? If you're ever faced with this situation, you need to do everything you can to change this perception. If the client does not provide resources to assist in the effort, then the probability of the project being unsuccessful increases significantly.

Projects require a team to deliver them successfully. Having the due diligence team, including the client, participate in the development ment will help ensure that there is buy-in from the individual team members on the process to be followed. It will also help ensure that no critical steps or data points are being overlooked.

> *Having the due diligence team, including the client, participate in the development will help ensure that there is buy-in from the individual team members on the process to be followed.*

Once the process overview has been completed and accepted by the team, the next step is to identify and collect the data to be analyzed. If an RFP is provided, this step may be as simple as identifying data from the document that need to be validated. If this is a noncompetitive bidding situation, then the team may need to go to the client and collect information specific to the engagement. However, use caution in accepting any data as factual without validation. RFPs are often developed very quickly by a single individual or team, who may not have coordinated with all the appropriate functional units in the organization. If the service provider submits a proposal based on inaccurate data, then the project is going to incur changes starting on day one.

After the data have been gathered, they should then be assessed and validated. To assess the data properly, the service provider will have to play the role of detective or investigator. This may require meeting with the various functional resources within the client organization. This role is particularly important when assessing processes and procedures. More than likely if a client is asking for help with developing new processes and procedures, the information provided in the RFP is limited. The individuals from the functional departments will likely have different perceptions of how the process actually works.

A good rule of thumb to use when assessing and validating information is to ask five people the same question about how something is defined or done within their organization. If all five answer the question the same way, then you can assume that the information is factual. If you get different answers, then additional investigation needs to be conducted.

After a thorough investigation of the data has been completed, the next step is to develop a gap analysis. The gap analysis documents the difference between the assumed data in an RFP or gathered as part of the sales process and the actual data found during the assessment and validation step. The simplest way to do this is by developing a matrix consisting of three columns: assumed, actual, and difference (or delta—Δ). This simple matrix will clearly illustrate the difference between what was originally assumed versus what was actually found in the client's environment.

Step 4: Develop the Due Diligence Report

Armed with the gap analysis from the assessment and validation step, the team can now develop the due diligence report. Although the report will be specific to the particular analysis conducted, some general headings can be used consistently. The following is a sample table of contents for a due diligence report:

Sample Due Diligence Report—Table of Contents

1. Introduction
1.1 Purpose
1.2 Scope of Analysis
1.3 Process Overview
1.4 Understanding the Current Environment
1.5 Deliverables
1.6 Key Recommendations

2. Analysis Section
2.1 Current Data or Process Analysis (including gap analysis)
2.2 Staffing Recommendations
2.3 Recommendations for Improvement
2.4 Process Work Flow Mapping (if applicable)

[A separate analysis section should be drafted for each critical data element or process being analyzed. Common subheadings, noted above, may be used under this category.]

3. General Recommendations
[The general recommendations section presents recommendations, and the corresponding benefits, that are not specific to a critical data element or service silo.]

4. Attachments
[This section provides all supporting documentation developed during the assessment and validation step.]

Once the report is finalized, it can be submitted to the client for consideration and approval. If a proposal has not been submitted, then the due diligence report will serve as the baseline document for the SOW. If the due diligence analysis follows the submission of a proposal and PSOW, then a formal change order will need to be requested to reflect the findings in the report. The client, the service provider, and any additional third-party contractors who may be impacted by the change should approve the change order. Once the change order has been approved, all appropriate documents should be revised to reflect the approved changes. This may be done by amending the PSOW with a copy of the approved change order.

Step 5: Evaluate and Control

As noted, due diligence may be conducted throughout the development of both the PSOW and the CSOW. Thus, it is important that a review process be established that will provide a mechanism for ensuring that the data upon which both the PSOW and CSOW are based are current and accurate. If a due diligence analysis was conducted after the proposal and PSOW were developed, then the initial analysis will serve as the foundation document for the data to be included in the CSOW. If the initial analysis was completed prior to the proposal being submitted, another analysis may need to be conducted prior to finalizing the CSOW.

The need to conduct a follow-up analysis may be contingent upon several factors, such as:

1. Scope changes were identified after the proposal was submitted.
2. Data upon which the proposal was based were found to be inaccurate or questionable.
3. Client requested an expeditious response to an RFP, not allowing sufficient time to plan the project properly during the proposal phase.

If changes are found during the evaluation, then the process is reiterated, starting with Step 2, developing the due diligence team. The purpose of starting with Step 2 is to ensure that the appropriate resources are available to assess and determine the validity of the new data. Establishing a periodic review or audit process will help identify changes that have occurred since the initial analysis. It will also help ensure that all critical data on the project are current and accurate. This will not only help expedite the development of the CSOW, but it will also be a significant factor in determining its quality.

BUILDING THE WORK BREAKDOWN STRUCTURE

Performing due diligence is the first step in forming the *foundation* for the SOW. The next step is to take the requirements definition and data gathered during due diligence and use them to develop a WBS for the project. The WBS is second only to the SOW in contributing to the successful delivery of a project. The reason it is second is that the SOW carries a contractual obligation with it that must be adhered to, whereas the WBS does not.

Evolution of the WBS

The genesis of most project management tools and techniques can be traced to DOD or NASA. This is also the case for the WBS. The WBS was first used in the late 1950s to graphically illustrate the evolution of the Program Evaluation Review Technique (PERT), which was developed by the U.S. Navy and the consulting firm Booz, Allen, Hamilton in developing time estimates for the activities to be performed on the Polaris Weapon System.[1,2] It wasn't until 1961 that the term *work breakdown structure* was formally recognized and commonly used in industry.[3] Since its formal recognition, it has become the *de facto* standard in both the public and private sectors for decomposing projects down to the lowest manageable level possible. This subdividing or decomposing of a project is critical in the development of the SOW. The more detailed the WBS, the more detailed the SOW.

NASA and DOD both cover the WBS in detail within their respective handbooks on the preparation of the SOW. As with the SOW, DOD is much more mature in the development and application of the WBS than most private sector firms. Its detailed handbook, *Department of Defense Handbook—Work Breakdown Structure* (MIL-HDBK-881, 2 January 1998), provides a standard approach for all DOD departments and agencies to follow in developing a WBS. (This handbook is provided for guidance only; developing a WBS is not a requirement for contracting with DOD.)

Having a consistent approach to developing the WBS has improved communication throughout the DOD acquisitions process. This handbook is specific to DOD, so not all of its concepts will be applicable to the private sector; nonetheless, there are lessons the private sector can learn from DOD's process. The most important lesson is the role and importance of the WBS in forming the foundation for the SOW. The quality of the SOW depends upon the quality of the WBS. If the WBS is poorly developed, then the SOW will not be at the level it needs to be to serve as a contractual document.

As the private sector becomes more mature in project management, it should also become more mature in developing WBSs for projects. This higher level of maturity in developing WBSs should also correlate to higher quality SOWs. Like DOD, every organization should have a customized process, specific to its environment, for developing a WBS. Having a standard approach will help build consistency in the way both the WBS and the SOW are prepared throughout the organization.

Defining the WBS

The Project Management Institute's *A Guide to the Project Management Body of Knowledge* (PMBOK®), 2000 edition, defines the WBS as "a deliverable-oriented grouping of project elements that organizes and defines the total work scope of the project. Each descending level represents an increasingly detailed definition of the project work."[4] The project elements can be either products or services. The WBS helps define and decompose (subdivide) the products or services into specific tasks, both managerial and technical, at various levels of detail. The more defined and detailed the decomposition, the greater the probability that all the major activities and tasks will be identified.

There is no standard one-size-fits-all WBS structure that is accepted unanimously by industry. Thus, it is typically up to the organization or the individual project manager to determine the structure and the level of detail of the WBS. The project may be subdivided down many levels, as long as the lowest level is still within the management authority of the project manager. For example, consider a PM who is managing the construction of a plane. The PM would be responsible for developing a WBS for the major elements of the plane, including the engine, wings, and fuselage. The PM, however, would not be concerned with the detailed WBS for the construction of these various components, since they are more than likely out of his or her area of control. In other words, the PM would not be concerned with the technical minutiae of all the activities and tasks required to construct a jet engine. The PM's focus would instead be on ensuring that these items are completed on time and within budget, so that they don't negatively impact the completion of the total product, in this case the plane.

The DOD WBS handbook (MIL-HDBK-881) addresses only the top three levels of the structure. It does not get into the multiple technical levels of the WBS that can occur on some projects. If your organization doesn't have an approved structure and guidelines for developing a WBS, you may want to consider using a six-level structure, which is a method frequently used in industry (see Figure 5-3).

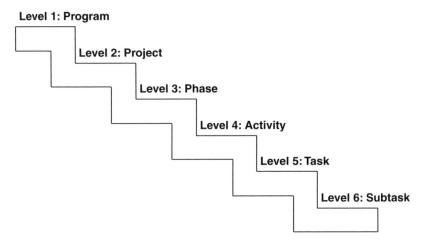

Figure 5-3. Six-Level WBS Structure

The six-level WBS can be displayed graphically as a hierarchy, or it can be shown in outline form, with the appropriate coding numbers, as shown in Figure 5-4.

The management levels will vary depending upon whether the engagement is classified as a program or a project. If it is a program, then the program manager will typically only be interested in the detail down to a Level 3. From a project standpoint, the project manager will be focused more on the detail down to Level 4. Levels 5 and 6 will be specific to the technical tasks and subtasks that need to be performed on the project. These elements may be assigned to a technical manager or lead to ensure that all the work is captured and performed correctly.

The term *work package* shown on Level 6 is defined as "a deliverable at the lowest level of the work breakdown structure, when that deliverable may be assigned to another project manager to plan and execute. This may be accomplished through the use of a subproject where the work package may be further decomposed into activities."[5] Although it is shown at the subtask level of the structure to illustrate its role in the WBS, it can actually exist anywhere below Level 3.

The benefits of having a good WBS include:

• Helps ensure that the requirements for the project are thoroughly defined

WBS Hierarchy

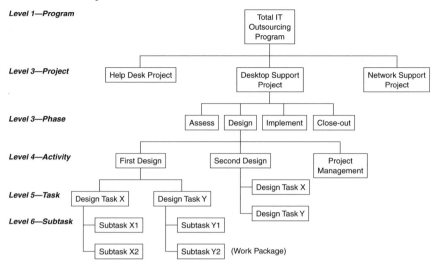

WBS Outline

1 Total IT Outsourcing Program
  1.1 Help Desk Project
  1.2 Desktop Support Project
    1.2.1 Assess
    1.2.2 Design
      1.2.2.1 First Design
        1.2.2.1.1 Design Task X
          1.2.2.1.1.1 Subtask X1
          1.2.2.1.1.2 Subtask X2
        1.2.2.1.2 Design Task Y
          1.2.2.1.2.1 Subtask Y1
          1.2.2.1.2.2 Subtask Y2
      1.2.2.2 Second Design
        1.2.2.2.1 Design Task X
        1.2.2.2.2 Design Task Y
      1.2.2.3 Project Management
    1.2.3 Implement
    1.2.4 Close-out
  1.3 Network Support Project

Figure 5-4. WBS Formats

- Makes drafting the SOW easier and provides part of the outline for the document
- Assists with developing proposal responses
- Assists the client in the evaluation and selection process.[6]

From a project management perspective, the WBS serves as a basis for other elements critical to the management of a project. These include:

- Organization breakdown structure (OBS)
- Responsibility assignment matrix (RAM)
- Precedence diagram for the schedule
- Risk analysis
- Cost estimate and budget
- Change control
- Schedule.

If the WBS is poorly done, this will ultimately affect the quality of each and every one of these elements and will damage the project or cause it to fail. Perhaps the best description of the WBS is that it's the aggregate that holds the foundation—of both the SOW and the project—together. Without the aggregate, the foundation will eventually crumble and fail.

Types of WBSs

As discussed in Chapter 3, there are primarily two types of SOWs: the proposal SOW (PSOW) and the contract SOW (CSOW). Since the WBS must be done prior to the SOW being developed, two forms of the WBS have to be developed: the proposal WBS (PWBS) and the contract WBS (CWBS).[7]

The PWBS is done as part of the proposal process. At this early stage, it may be feasible only to go down to a Level 3 or 4. The PWBS is typically done in competitive bidding situations, where the response time is very short and limited time is available for planning. In these situations, it is important that time be allowed between acceptance of the proposal by the client and execution of the contract to perform the due diligence analysis. This will help bring the content up to a level where it can be considered a CWBS. If the service provider is forced to sign a contract based on a PWBS and a PSOW, then it is critical that a change management plan be in place and understood by the client because changes will begin to be made on day one.

The CWBS is the WBS that is developed to the lowest level of detail as defined by the sponsoring organization. This means that if the organization is using the six-level structure, then the WBS should be developed all the way down to the sixth level. If the team is unable to define the project to this lowest level, this should be recognized as one of the first indications that either the project scope has not been clearly defined or that the resources assigned to the project do not have the appropriate expertise or knowledge about the work to properly define it. Either way, it should raise a red flag to the project manager and the appropriate stakeholders. The ultimate goal of the CWBS is to define the project in as much detail as possible, without getting into minutiae that are beyond the control of the PM.

Developing the WBS

The first step in developing a WBS is to write a clear statement of the objective for the proposed work. (This might have been completed as part of the due diligence analysis.) The next step is to have the team, preferably a TIGER team, subdivide the work into activities, tasks, and subtasks according to the six-level structure.

One of the most popular methods used to facilitate this process is the Post-it® Notes method. When using the Post-it® Notes method, it is important that the team developing the WBS meet in a project or meeting room that has a large blank wall. Using the six-level structure as a guideline, the team brainstorms about all the activities, tasks, and subtasks required to deliver the project successfully. Each work element is then be drafted on a Post-it® and placed on the wall. (It's important that the team not try to identify the successor and predecessor relationships of these elements at this point because it could inhibit them from identifying all the required elements.)

Once it is agreed that all the elements have been identified, the team can then group the elements into their respective silos. This is where the Post-it® Notes come in handy, because they can easily be moved around to the appropriate location. Also, if gaps are identified, new elements can be documented very quickly on a Post-it® and placed in the appropriate location. Once all work elements have been properly grouped, any duplication or redundancy should be eliminated from the structure. The predecessor and successor relationships between the various elements can then be established.

Several software packages are currently available on the market that can assist with developing the WBS. One of the best is WBS Chart Pro®, which is produced by Critical Tools® (www.criticaltools.com). This tool provides an electronic version of the Post-it® Note method, only with a lot more functionality. It also seamlessly integrates with Microsoft Project® for easy development of the schedule.

The following guidelines can assist in development of the WBS:

- Ensure that the appropriate resources participate in the development, preferably a TIGER team.
- Develop the WBS structure by decomposing the project into discrete and logical elements of work (e.g., activities, tasks, subtasks).
- Ensure that the next lower level of the decomposition represents 100 percent of the work and cost at the next corresponding higher level (i.e., 100 percent rule).[8]
- Ensure that the WBS satisfies all managerial and technical requirements of the project.
- Avoid getting so detailed in the decomposition that the WBS becomes unmanageable.
- Ensure that each work package has a specific deliverable associated with it and that the work can be assigned to one person.
- Avoid duplication and redundancy of work elements in the WBS.
- Ensure that the project management activities are addressed on every WBS.
- The sequence of the work is not important as long as there is some logic to the structure. (Sequencing and relationships—predecessors and successors—will be established later in the process.)
- For solicitation purposes, the WBS generally does not have to go lower than the top three or four levels, depending on whether the initiative is considered a program or a project.

Following these simple guidelines will help provide a structure for developing the WBS on future projects. If you or your organization is not currently following a consistent approach, this will help you take the first step toward establishing consistency, which should lead to higher quality WBSs on future projects.

Relationship between the WBS and the SOW

The next step in the WBS process is defining its relationship to the SOW. Some literature recommends that the WBS be used to establish the outline of the SOW.[9] However, this can be very confusing and misleading to someone who has never developed an SOW before. If one were simply to take the WBS outline and make it the outline for the SOW, a great deal of information would not captured. The more appropriate guidance is to use the WBS outline to develop the outline or table of contents for the technical or functional requirements contained in the SOW. Moreover, if the WBS were used to develop the outline of the SOW, then the structure of every SOW an organization did would be different. As we'll see in Chapter 6, one way to address this issue is to establish a consistent structure for the SOW, with certain sections having the flexibility to be customized to the particular project. The WBS structure can then be integrated within these sections while maintaining a standard framework.

The evolution of project data from the initial requirements definition through the development of the SOW can be depicted as follows:

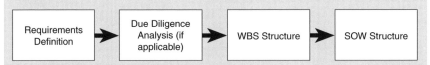

This evolution is what forms and builds the foundation for the SOW. Without this process, the data supporting the SOW may be corrupted or not of the quality desired. Following this process will help form and build a solid foundation for the SOW, which will contribute significantly to the ultimate success of the project.

NOTES

[1]Gregory T. Haugan. *Effective Work Breakdown Structures* (Vienna, VA: Management Concepts, Inc., 2002).

[2]Harold Kerzner, Ph.D., *Project Management: A Systems Approach to Planning, Scheduling, and Controlling*, 5th ed. (New York: Van Nostrand Reinhold, 1995), p. 654.

[3]Haugan, p. 8.

[4]Project Management Institute, *A Guide to the Project Management Body of Knowledge* (PMBOK® Guide–2000 Edition) (Newtown Square, PA: Project Management Institute 2000), p. 209.

[5]Ibid.

[6]NASA Handbook 5600.2A–*Statements of Work Handbook*, 23 July 1993, p. 28.

[7]Kerzner, pp. 535–536.

[8]Haugan, p. 17.

[9]Kerzner, p. 538.

Chapter 6
Framing the SOW

What one man does, another fails to do: what's fit for me may not be fit for you.

—*Anonymous*

An SOW framework that may be appropriate and applicable in one organization may not be appropriate and applicable in another. Once the initial data have been gathered and the foundation has been established, the next step is to develop and customize the framework of the SOW specific to the client or project that it is supporting. A customized framework will help organize the content into areas of information and thus allow the development team to identify and assign the appropriate resources to specific sections. This will make it easier for the team to draft the content, in turn reducing the likelihood of duplication and redundancy. Having the document organized into a clear and concise framework will

> *A customized framework will help organize the content into areas of information and thus allow the development team to identify and assign the appropriate resources to specific sections.*

also allow the reader to review and understand its contents more easily, which will help avoid any misinterpretations or misperceptions.

While a single comprehensive framework is not applicable for all projects, a baseline framework consisting of key elements can serve as a starting point for an SOW in any organization or project. For this baseline framework to be useful and flexible, it has to have both *static* and *dynamic* characteristics. It must be *static* in that all sections of the framework have to be addressed for every engagement, regardless of the type of project being performed. It must be *dynamic* in that the content within the sections can be customized or new sections added to the framework to fit the needs and requirements of the client or project.

Framing the SOW is the second step of the F3 methodology for building the foundation for successful projects. This step plays an important role in building consistency and improving the quality of SOWs developed within an organization. The following guidelines will assist in developing the framework properly and will provide a detailed description of the key elements making up that framework.

DEVELOPING THE SOW FRAMEWORK

One of the most common frustrations for someone who is developing an SOW for the first time is determining where to start. This is particularly true for individuals or teams in organizations that are at a low level of maturation in the discipline of project management. For the most part, the literature recommends using the WBS to structure the SOW.[1] However, if you follow this approach, the final SOW will be very limited in describing what is to be provided to the client as well as what is required by the service provider to deliver the product or service. Because the WBS focuses on the deliverables to be provided to the client, it does not include all integral elements required by the service provider to deliver the project successfully.

The SOW is both a management and a contractual document. Therefore, it is important that both the organization's project management directorate and its legal department develop and approve the baseline framework. The project management directorate should ensure that those elements required to manage and deliver the project successfully are captured in the document. The legal department will be focused primarily on ensuring that the framework and content contained within the SOW comply with the organization's standard legal terms and conditions (Ts & Cs) and do not include contradictory or duplicate information. Taking the time to ensure that the SOW does not duplicate or conflict with the content of the legal Ts & Cs will help avoid potential litigation later on.

The framework of the PSOW is the baseline for the development of the CSOW. As noted, the information contained in a PSOW will generally be at a very high level. This may be sufficient for an initial proposal response, but it will be insufficient to serve as the basis for a contract. The CSOW, on the other hand, will ideally be finalized following a due diligence analysis of the data supporting it, as well as the development of a detailed or contract work breakdown structure (CWBS). This analysis and additional planning will allow the team to develop a CSOW, which, when completed, will be more detailed than the PSOW.

Using the same framework for each type of SOW will allow the development team to readily determine what has or hasn't changed since the initial proposal response. This is also critical from a knowledge management standpoint in that the ability to compare the PSOW to the CSOW will provide future SOW development teams with critical information on how best to structure and detail the document. It will also help refine and improve the due diligence analysis, which in turn will allow the organization to determine which process and data elements provide the greatest benefits in forming the foundation of the SOW.

Using the same framework for each type of SOW will allow the development team to readily determine what has or hasn't changed since the initial proposal response.

The ultimate goal is to continually refine the framework and content of the SOW for specific types of projects to such a degree that there is very little difference between the PSOW and the CSOW. In effect, you are developing boilerplate information that can easily be replicated for projects similar in nature and scope. Further, getting the documents as close as possible to each other in structure and content will help the service provider respond more expeditiously and accurately in competitive bidding situations. This is particularly useful when a quick response turnaround is important. It will also result in more accurate cost, schedule, and manpower estimates in the PSOW, thus reducing the number of change orders that occur during the life of the project.

STRUCTURE OF THE BASELINE SOW FRAMEWORK

Developing a standard framework for an SOW is not an easy process. No single framework is applicable to every industry, organization, and project. What may work well for one organization and industry may not work well for another. Nonetheless, a baseline framework that has both *static* and *dynamic* characteristics can generally provide a starting point for any industry, organization, and project. This standard baseline SOW framework includes:

- Table of Contents
- Statement of Confidentiality
- Introduction
- Services (or Products) Provided
- Roles and Responsibilities
- Management Procedures
- Hours of Operation
- Facilities/Tools/Equipment Requirements
- Schedule
- Pricing
- Signature Block
- Glossary of Terms
- Attachments.

These sections may be stand-alone elements, or they may act as summary headings over multiple subsections that address the element in more detail. Other sections, which may not be included as part of the standard baseline framework but are commonly used in outsourcing or professional services engagements, include:

- Service Responsibility Transfer
- Security Requirements
- Marketing Requirements.

In some cases, a section of the baseline framework may not apply to a particular project or client. In these situations, the development team would simply address the section as being "not applicable" (N/A). It is important that every section of the baseline framework be addressed, whether it applies or not. This ensures that nothing has been overlooked during the development. In other cases, additional sections may be necessary to fully capture all client and service provider requirements to deliver the project successfully. These sections would simply be added to the baseline framework and ultimately become part of the CSOW for the project. Any sections labeled N/A can be eliminated from the document prior to finalizing the CSOW.

Determining the outline format or *coding* structure is the next step in framing the SOW. Coding is the numerical outline of the sections making up the SOW. As noted, some literature recommends using the WBS coding structure to format the SOW. An example of the coding structure for a six-level WBS is presented in Figure 6-1.

Using the WBS coding structure is easier said than done. By definition, the SOW is "a narrative description of the products and services to be supplied to the client and the needs and requirements of the contractor to deliver such products and services properly under the contract." Thus, the SOW is focused on more than just the deliverables being supplied to the client. It also takes into consideration the needs and requirements of the service provider. The WBS, however, is focused on the deliverables and doesn't take into consideration the other elements required to deliver the project. The structure of the WBS doesn't allow for easy translation into the structure of the SOW, particularly when an organization lacks a consistent approach or method for developing a WBS.

Once the WBS is completed, it is used to develop the schedule for the project, which then becomes the primary tool that the project manager uses to manage day-to-day project activities. Once the schedule has been developed, the WBS is seldom revisited during the project. If the WBS is not updated every time a change occurs on the project, then it becomes inconsistent with the SOW. On the other hand, if the WBS were maintained and updated appropriately, then the coding

LEVEL	WBS CODING STRUCTURE
1—Program	1.0
2—Project	1.1
3—Phase	1.1.1
4—Activity	1.1.1.1
5—Task	1.1.1.1.1
6—Subtask	1.1.1.1.1.1

Figure 6-1. Coding Structure for a Six-Level WBS

structure could potentially be revised every time a change occurred. If the coding structure for the WBS changed, then the SOW coding structure would also have to be changed to maintain consistency. Trying to maintain consistency of the content and format between the WBS and the SOW would be a management nightmare. The solution is to apply a unique coding structure specific to the standard baseline framework without consideration of the WBS outline. The WBS would still be used in identifying and structuring the content to be addressed in the services or products section of the baseline framework.

A numerical hierarchical approach should be used as the coding structure for the SOW. The coding would be applied first to the Statement of Confidentiality section, which would be coded as Section 1. Each of the following sections would then be coded in ascending order up to the last section, which in this case would be Section 12—Attachments. The number of sections in the final CSOW will depend on whether any sections have been added to or deleted from the baseline framework.

Benefits realized from using the baseline framework with its own unique coding structure include:

- Provides a standard framework for developing SOWs within an organization
- Helps build consistency in structure and content
- Improves the quality of SOWs being developed
- Reduces the difficulty of managing changes made to the project and, in turn, to the SOW, during project execution
- Permits better knowledge management and transfer of information for future projects.

Following the recommended coding, a detailed description of the recommended sections for the baseline SOW framework and their content are as follows:

Table of Contents: Every SOW longer than two pages should have a table of contents (TOC).[2] The TOC should document all primary sections of the baseline SOW framework, as well as any additional sections that may be required for a particular client or project. The TOC should also list supporting attachments and appendices.

1.0—Statement of Confidentiality: This section addresses the confidentiality of the SOW to ensure that the client understands that unauthorized duplication or distribution of the information in the document is not permitted. This includes protection for any techniques, methodologies, and processes included in the SOW that the service provider may consider confidential and proprietary. The statement of confidentiality is of particular importance in the PSOW, during which there is no contractual obligation between the client and the service provider. The information at this point is not secure and is susceptible to misuse by either the client or another service provider.

2.0—Introduction: The introduction consists of several subsections, including *purpose, description of work, assumptions, and constraints*. In situations where subsections are required, the coding structure should follow an ascending order similar to that of the overall baseline framework.

- **2.1—*Purpose***: This subsection describes the purpose of the SOW and the project it is supporting. It generally consists of only a couple of sentences or paragraphs, but it may be expanded to include a statement of the problem (i.e., the reason the project is being initiated). If the section is expanded, it should define the problem that is driving the need for the proposed project, the client's goals, and the role of the service provider in helping the client achieve those goals.
- **2.2—*Description of Work***: This is a written description of the scope of work to be performed. The description provides a summary of the services or products to be provided, with reference to the section number described in the framework. This subsection is generally no longer than one page and in most cases consists of a couple of paragraphs. It should describe the output, approach, and content of the project to help establish a common understanding of the project's scope by all stakeholders.[3]

This section should not cover elements considered to be out-

> *Anything that is not covered within the text of the SOW should be considered out-of-scope.*

side the scope of the project. Anything that is not covered within the text of the SOW should be considered out-of-scope. Anything that is added to the scope later can be done through the change management process.

- **2.3—*Assumptions*:** Assumptions are data elements or factors that are considered to be true or factual and are used as part of the decision-making process. An assumption may be based on information provided by the client or obtained as part of a preliminary evaluation. If an assumption is found to be incorrect during the due diligence analysis or in the delivery of the services or product, then a change order should be processed immediately to reflect the actual information. The assumptions section should not be finalized until the SOW has been completed because as the SOW is being developed, the team may uncover and identify gaps in the document (i.e., insufficient data to move forward with the execution of a contract). If this is the case, then assumptions will need to be made and documented by the development team to compensate for these gaps. It is further recommended that this section be reserved for those assumptions that are general or universal in nature relative to a particular client or project. Assumptions specific to a product or service should be identified in Section 3 of the baseline framework.

- **2.4—*Constraints*:** This section describes all constraints that may negatively impact the successful completion of a project. A constraint is defined as any event or situation that may:
  - Prevent the service provider from delivering the services or products required
  - Limit the availability of alternative solutions
  - Inhibit the client from meeting its obligations.

  A similar but slightly more detailed definition is as follows:

  "(1) Restriction that affects the scope of the project, usually with regard to availability, assignment, or use of project cost, schedule, or resources.

  (2) Any factor that affects when or how an activity can be scheduled.

  (3) Any factor that limits the project team's options and can lead to pressure and resulting frustrations among team members."[4]

  Constraints on a project may include budget, security, facility, geography, and resources. Any constraint identified during the development of the SOW must be considered a potential risk, and mitigation plans should be developed as a preventive measure.

3.0—Services (or Products) Provided: This section addresses in detail each product or service to be provided to the client. As such, it is the most dynamic section of the entire framework. A separate subsection should be included for each service or product being provided to the client. As noted in Section 2, the coding of the subsections should follow an ascending order similar to that of the overall baseline framework. For instance, the subsections for three services to be provided to a client could be coded as follows:

3.1—Help Desk Services
3.2—Network Support Services
3.3—Business Process Re-engineering Services.

The following information should be captured for each product or service being provided to the client:

- *Description*: This provides a detailed written description of the product or service to be provided to the client. The description should be as detailed as possible, without overspecifying. This section should not exceed more than a few paragraphs; however, the length will often be contingent upon the technical difficulty of the product or service being delivered. Keep in mind that the description should address only *what* is being provided to the client, not *how* it's being delivered. Any "how to" requirements should not be included in the SOW since the service provider should only be tasked to provide the deliverables under the contract in the most cost-effective manner possible.[5] Also, as noted in Section 2.2, address only the elements of the service or product that are in scope. Do not attempt to document elements considered to be out of scope.
- *Key assumptions*: These are assumptions specific to the product or service being delivered to the client. Reference the definition for assumptions in Section 2.
- *Roles and Responsibilities*: Identify the roles and responsibilities of the service provider, client, and any third parties specific to each product or service being delivered.
- *Change Enablement*: This captures all elements required to support the implementation of a product or service within a client's

environment. This includes requirements such as training and communications specific to implementation.

- *Service Level Agreements (SLAs)*: SLAs specify service levels required by the client. Service levels are quantitative measures, established or requested by the client, upon which the performance of the service provider will be measured. In a direct marketing effort or noncompetitive bidding process, the service provider may also propose the service level to the client. An example of a service level for help desk services may be that first call resolution must average 65 percent over the life of the project. If this average percentage is not achieved for first call resolution, then the client is going to be dissatisfied and the service provider may incur significant financial penalties. Service levels may be addressed in the section specific to a particular service, or they may be captured in a separate section, which would identify the SLAs for all services being delivered. The recommended approach, however, is to identify the SLAs within the section describing the service being delivered. Doing this will keep all information specific to a service in one location.

- *Key Requirements*: This describes all specific requirements requested by the client. This will often pertain more to the delivery of a product than to a service. Unlike service levels, which identify a quantitative performance target against which the service provider is to be measured, the requirements section identifies specific characteristics that a product must have for it to be acceptable to the client. For example, a client may have a requirement that a customized software package being developed have the capability of integrating with its current legacy systems.

- *Deliverables*: Any required deliverables that are specific to the service or product being delivered to the client should be addressed in this section. The development team may choose to address *all* deliverables in a separate section. However, it is strongly recommended that if multiple services or products are being provided, the deliverables be clearly defined within the section specific to the service or product to which they apply. It's also important that this section clearly define the client's acceptance criteria for each deliverable required for the project.

Constraints are generally not addressed as part of this section, since they tend to be more global in nature than specific to a particular product or service. However, if a constraint is specific to a product or service, then it should be addressed in the section addressing that product or service.

4.0—Roles and Responsibilities: This section addresses the roles and responsibilities of the service provider, the client, and any additional third parties that have not been addressed in the services or product section. This section tends to be more focused on the roles and responsibilities at the executive level of these parties. An example would be defining the roles and responsibilities of an executive steering committee for the project.

5.0—Management Procedures: This section addresses the processes and procedures for managing the delivery of the product or service to the client. It does not describe the specific aspects of *how* a product or service is going to be developed or implemented. Rather, it focuses specifically on the management aspect of certain processes and procedures that are required to manage the SOW and deliver the project successfully to the client. The processes and procedures covered in this section would include:

- Change control process
- Billing process
- Dispute resolution process
- Reporting procedure
  - Status reports
  - Client satisfaction reports
- Meetings.

Any process flow diagrams associated with or supporting these various management elements may be included in the attachments to the SOW.

6.0—Hours of Operation: This section addresses the hours the service provider will, or will not, perform services or charge to the development of a product. The hours of operation may be defined by service, product type, or location/site. This section should clearly define overtime, holidays, and after-hours work. It is also important that the time be specific to a time zone, particularly if work is being conducted across multiple geographic locations and time zones.

In describing the hours of operation, it is extremely important that the limits of the business day be clearly defined. For example, is the business day defined as being 8 hours, 10 hours, or 24 hours? Clearly communicating and understanding what constitutes a business day is a very important element in the development of both the SOW and the schedule. If this is not clearly defined, it could lead to misinterpretation and confusion about how much it will cost to deliver the product or service as well as when it is scheduled to be completed.

7.0—Facilities/Tools/Equipment Requirements: This section describes the facilities, tools, and equipment that the service provider requires to deliver the product or service properly. This is one of the most overlooked areas of an SOW, yet it can be one of the most critical in delivering a project successfully. If the client is unable to provide adequate facilities, tools, and equipment, then it can be almost impossible for the service provider to be successful.

A common complaint by service providers once they've won a project and they're on site is that they don't have adequate facilities or access to the proper tools and equipment for their personnel to deliver the services properly. Not only is it difficult to deliver the services or products when these items aren't provided, but it can also lead to a rapid deterioration of employee morale. People naturally migrate to situations that make their jobs easier and more enjoyable and away from those that make their job more difficult and less enjoyable. Properly identifying all necessary and required facilities, tools, and equipment in the SOW can help mitigate against this situation.

Guidelines for accurately capturing the appropriate information in this section include:

- Describe the location where facilities, tools, or equipment will be required. This includes identifying the specific office and geographic location at which a product or service is being provided.
- Identify the size, type, and numbers of the items required. For example, if office space is required, the service provider should document the square footage needed, as well as whether the space should be a separate office, cubicle, meeting room, or storage space.
- Define infrastructure requirements, such as security clearance, building access, network access, telephone access, climate con-

trol, furniture, lockable storage, wastebaskets, and coat racks. (The reason for this level of detail is covered in Chapter 8.)
- Define administrative facilities and tool requirements such as document reproduction, office supplies, and kitchen/food facilities.
- Define parking requirements.
- Clearly specify that any facilities provided should meet the Americans with Disabilities Act of 1990 and the Occupational Safety and Health Act of 1970. (This requirement may be captured in the legal terms and conditions instead.)

8.0—Schedule: The schedule for delivering the product or service to the client should be based on the WBS (the PWBS for a PSOW and the CWBS for the CSOW). It should identify only major milestones and their scheduled completion dates, against which progress can be measured throughout the life of the project. The full schedule may be included as an attachment to the SOW.

9.0—Pricing: The pricing structure for delivering the product or service to the client can be segmented into various categories, including:

- Initial ramp-up and one-time fees
- Base fees
- Time and materials
- Travel and expenses
- Mailing fees
- Third-party expenses
- Acquisition fees (if applicable)
- Termination fees.

10.0—Signature Block: This section captures the signatures of all representatives, from both the service provider and the client, responsible for approving the SOW. Having the client sign off on the document will show its agreement to the scope of the project as described.

11.0—Glossary of Terms: This section addresses the agreed-upon definitions of the concepts, words, and phrases used in the text of the SOW. Having a detailed glossary will eliminate any misinterpretation and avoid ambiguity.

12.0—Attachments: This section contains all additional information referenced in the SOW, including items such as:

- Detailed schedule
- Change order form (with instructions)
- Process flow diagrams (referenced in the management procedures section)
- Sample reports.

Other sections that may be included as part of the standard baseline SOW framework for outsourcing and professional service organizations are as follows:

Service (or Product) Responsibility Transfer: This section addresses the requirements that need to be met to ensure a smooth transition between the incoming and outgoing service providers and the client. This section is of particular importance in outsourcing projects. For these types of projects, this section may address issues such as:

- Hiring displaced employees from the current service provider, which may be internal or external to the client
- Transfer of responsibilities and facilities from the team currently performing services to the new team.

Security Requirements: This section addresses the client's security requirements, as well as the roles and responsibilities of both the client and the service provider in meeting these requirements. If the client requires security clearance, it should assume the cost of the service provider meeting these requirements. This section should include:

- Identification of all secure locations, which would include sites such as nuclear power facilities, top secret facilities, and executive areas.
- Identification of all security requirements that must be met to deliver services properly, including background investigations and drug screening.
- Agreement of the client to identify and provide appropriate security clearance. If the appropriate clearance is not identified and provided, then the service provider should not be held accountable for meeting the SLAs.

Marketing Requirements: This section addresses the marketing effort undertaken with the client to ensure awareness of the product or services being implemented or made available to the organization. An example is a project in which a new computer operating system is being implemented firmwide. To implement this new system properly, all employees may be required to perform some initial tasks in preparing for the upgrade. The employees may also need to receive training on how to use the new system. This section would address how this guidance will be communicated to the organization and the stakeholders. It will also identify who is responsible for the cost of the marketing effort. Methods of communicating a new product or service may include:

- Newsletters
- E-mail
- Posters
- Mouse pads
- T-shirts.

Overlooking this section could negatively impact both the client and the service provider financially. For example, a sales manager on one project I'm familiar with promised the client that the service provider would provide all employees with a mouse pad announcing a new service being offered within the client organization. However, neither the sales manager nor the client had budgeted for this expense, which amounted to approximately $90,000. Since the sales manager for the service provider had made the commitment, the service provider ended up eating the cost. Needless to say, all future SOWs developed by this organization included a section on marketing requirements.

The following guidelines summarize key aspects in the development and application of a standard baseline SOW framework:

- Every project will need an SOW customized specifically for the client and the project the document is supporting.
- Every SOW developed by an organization must follow the current baseline SOW framework approved by both the project management directorate and the legal department.

- Sections may be added to the SOW; however, no section should be eliminated from the approved format until the CSOW has been finalized.
- The development team should address each section of the baseline framework. If a particular section doesn't apply, then it should still be addressed by identifying that it's not applicable (N/A) for that engagement.
- Prior to finalizing the CSOW, those sections that have been identified as N/A can be eliminated from the document.

NOTES

[1]Harold Kerzner, Ph.D., *Project Management: A Systems Approach to Planning, Scheduling, and Controlling,* 5th ed. (New York: Van Nostrand Reinhold, 1995), p. 583.

[2]Ibid., p. 586.

[3]J. LeRoy Ward, *Project Management Terms—A Working Glossary* (Arlington, VA: ESI International, 1997).

[4]Ibid., p. 30.

[5]Department of Defense, *Handbook for Preparation of Statement of Work* (SOW), MIL-HDBK-245D, 3 April 1996, p. 9.

Chapter 7
Finalizing the SOW

The difference between the almost right word and the right word is really a large matter—it's the difference between the lightning bug and lightning.
—Mark Twain

The third and final phase of the F3 methodology is the *finalizing* phase. During this phase, the development team will start writing content for the various sections of the SOW. The successful completion of this phase depends largely upon the quality of the information and data gathered and developed during the *foundation* and *framing* phases. Obtaining detailed, quality data during the foundation phase will help ensure that the content of the CSOW will be accurate and valid. In addition, if the structure of the SOW is well defined and organized, it will be much easier for the development team to follow. It will also help ensure that the appropriate team members are assigned to the sections of the document that best match their area of expertise.

It is imperative that the SOW be organized and written clearly to avoid any misinterpretation or confusion among the parties who will be referring to it throughout the life of the project and to help the delivery team manage changes that occur during project implementation.

> *It is imperative that the SOW be organized and written clearly to avoid any misinterpretation or confusion among the parties who will be referring to it throughout the life of the project.*

Completing the *finalizing* phase of the SOW entails more than just drafting the document; it also addresses the SOW's role in developing the cost of the project as well as its role in negotiating the contract between the service provider and the client.

DRAFTING A QUALITY SOW

In drafting the SOW, it doesn't matter what the author meant to say, what was understood, or what was spoken; it only matters how the document reads. Writing is a tangible, lasting form of communication, which allows the reader to hold it, look at it, contemplate it, reference it, save it, and interpret it. Other forms of communication, such as body language or the spoken word, do not allow the recipient the same level of analysis that the written word provides.

Although communication is an important objective of writing, it is not the only one. Howard and Barton propose that "the first goal of writing, like reading, is to understand; only then can one make that understanding available to others in writing."[1] This is first establishing one's thoughts, and then *re*-establishing these thoughts in written form to communicate the intent of the message. If these thoughts are not articulated well, then the message will not be communicated successfully to the reader. Similarly, if the SOW is drafted in such a way that it confuses or misleads the reader, then the likelihood of the project being unsuccessful increases significantly. Thus, it is imperative that the development team understand the importance of writing an SOW that clearly articulates what is to be provided to the client and what the service provider requires to deliver the services or product.

> *In drafting the SOW, it doesn't matter what the author meant to say, what was understood, or what was spoken; it only matters how the document reads.*

The SOW will be read and used by a diverse group that includes individuals from varied backgrounds and disciplines, including engineers, attorneys, contract personnel, accountants, technical specialists, and cost estimators. The SOW should be written clearly and concisely in such a way that each representative from these various disciplines can easily understand the intent of the text without requiring interpretation. There are some do's and don'ts of writing a quality SOW.

Do's:

1. **Use simple and direct language for clarity**: Sentences should be as short and concise as possible, without sacrificing clarity. The language should be free from all vague and ambiguous terms and should be easily understandable to all potential stakeholders. The SOW should be written in such a way that nothing in it is open to interpretation. Words such as *shall* and *will* fit these criteria. The word *shall* indicates that a requirement identified in the SOW is mandatory and binding. For example, "The service provider *shall* deliver the product within 30 days of the contract execution date." The word *will* may indicate a declaration on the part of either the service provider or the client that something will be performed or delivered. For example, "The client *will* provide the service provider with a 10' x 30' work space for its staff." The words *might, may,* and *should* do not convey this same type of directness, which is required for the SOW. They infer a degree of flexibility and lack of enforcement that either the service provider or the client may misinterpret; thus, they should not be used in the SOW.

2. **Use the active voice:** The SOW should be written in the active voice rather than the passive voice. Active voice implies strength, directness, and clarity; the passive voice is weak and can lead to vague statements that may be open to misinterpretation. The following sentences illustrate this point:

   Passive Voice—"A customized software package for Client #1 is being developed by Company Z."
   Active Voice—"Company Z is developing a customized software package for Client #1."

   Active work words, which convey a form of action or work function, should be used to help ensure that the conciseness and clarity of the content are maintained. A list of active work words is provided in Figure 7-1.[2]

3. **Use positive and specific words and phrases:** In writing the SOW, every effort should be made to draft the content using positive words, even when an element may be negative. Negative words such as *do not, cannot,* and *will not* should be avoided. For example:

Work Word	Meaning
analyze	solve by analysis
annotate	provide with comments
ascertain	find out with certainty
attend	be present at
audit	officially examine
build	make by putting together
calculate	find out by computation
compare	find out likenesses or differences
consider	think about, decide
construct	put together, build
control	direct, regulate
contribute	give along with others
define	make clear, set the limits
design	perform an original act
determine	resolve, settle, decide
develop	bring into being or activity
differentiate	make a distinction between
erect	put together, set upright
establish	set up, settle, prove beyond dispute
estimate	approximate an opinion of
evaluate	find or fix the value of
evolve	develop gradually, work out
examine	look at closely, test quality of
explore	examine for discovery
extract	take out, deduce, select
fabricate	build, manufacture, invent
form	give shape to, establish
formulate	put together, add, express
generate	produce, cause to be
identify	show or find
implement	carry out, put into practice
inquire	ask, make a search of
inspect	examine carefully or officially
install	place, put into position
institute	set up, establish, begin

Figure 7-1. Active Work Words

Work Word	Meaning
integrate	to add parts to make whole
interpret	explain the meaning of
investigate	search into, examine closely
judge	decide, form an estimate
maintain	keep in an existing state, continue
make	cause to come into being
manufacture	fabricate from raw materials
modify	change, alter
monitor	watch or observe
notice	comment upon, review
observe	inspect, watch
originate	initiate, give rise to
organize	integrate, arrange in a coherent unit
perform	do, carry out, accomplish
plan	devise a scheme for doing, making; arrange activities to achieve
probe	investigate thoroughly
produce	give birth or rise to
pursue	seek, obtain, or accomplish
reason	think, influence another's actions
recommend	advise, attract favor of
record	set down in writing, or act of electronic reproduction of communication
resolve	reduce by analysis, clear up
review	inspection, examination, or evaluation
revise	correct, improve
scan	look through hastily, examine intently
screen	separate, present, or shield
search	examine to find something
seek	try to discover, make an attempt
solve	find an answer
test	evaluate, examine
trace	copy or find by searching
track	observe or plot the path of
update	modernize, make current

Figure 7-1. Active Work Words (continued)

"The service provider *will not* deliver help desk services on the weekend." (Negative)

"The service provider *will* deliver help desk services every weekday." (Positive)

Negative words and phrases typically have the word "not" in them. A quick review of the SOW can identify these words. The development team can then replace these with positive words and phrases. The following list illustrates how a single word can easily be substituted for a negative phrase to transform it into a positive form (or at least less negative!). [3]

Negative Phrase	Positive Word
do not go fast	> slow down
do not remember	> forget
not possible	> impossible
not known	> unknown
not sure	> unsure

4. **Use technical language sparingly:** If the SOW is supporting a technical project, it may be necessary to use some technical language throughout the text to convey the intent of the work to be performed. However, every effort should be made to use the technical language sparingly and defer to simple wording in concise sentences as much as possible. When considering whether technical language should be used, the development team should consider whether the audience who will be reading the document will understand its meaning and application. If not everyone will understand the technical application, then the team *must* take special precautions to draft it in layman terms. Another option for the development team would be to reference the technical design or similar document that the readers may refer to if they want more information or further explanation of the technical aspects of the project.

5. **Define acronyms and abbreviations:** Ensure that all acronyms and abbreviations are spelled out the first time they are used and shown in parentheses after the spelled-out phrases. It is also important that each acronym and abbreviation be defined in the SOW glossary.[4] This will provide the reader with a single point

of reference to confirm the definition or meaning of words or phrases.

6. **General writing considerations:** It is extremely important that the document be as easy to read as possible. Consider these general guidelines in writing the SOW:

- Use 8½" x 11," letter size paper.
- Allow sufficient and consistent margins, preferably at least one inch on every side of the page.
- Use an easy-to-read font type and size. Times New Roman, 12 pt. font will work well in most cases.
- For the initial drafts, the lines of text should be double-spaced. This will allow for easier reading and provide the review team with room to make comments. (If the SOW is unusually long and there's a need to reduce the number of pages, the development team may choose to use single-spacing.)
- For the initial drafts, each line should be numbered. This allows the review team to reference their comments directly to a line number in the document, rather than having to reference it to a section number, paragraph, and sentence. The line numbers may be removed from the final draft, which will be referenced in the contract.

Don'ts

1. **Don't use vague or obscure words and phrases with multiple or legal meanings:** Ambiguity is one of the leading causes of deficient SOWs. Ambiguity occurs when terms that have two or more possible meanings are used or when their meaning is vague, indefinite, or uncertain.[5] Common words that may cause a sentence or phrase to be ambiguous include:

- best effort
- adequate
- excessive
- high quality
- reasonably
- similar
- etc.

Legal words and phrases may also lead to ambiguity. These include:

- partnership
- alliance
- guaranty
- insure
- ensure
- assure
- warranty
- warrant.

Phrases that have multiple meanings and that should therefore be avoided when drafting an SOW are listed in Figure 7-2.[6]

If the meaning of the text is unclear to the reader, then the likelihood of it being misinterpreted by the service provider, client, or any other involved party greatly increases. To illustrate how an ambiguous statement can creep into the SOW, consider a scenario in which the service provider requires workspace within the client's organization to be able to deliver a specific service. The following sentences illustrate both an ambiguous statement and the correct method for documenting this requirement within the SOW:

1. "The client will provide *adequate* space to the service provider through the term of this contract." (*Ambiguous*)
2. "The client will provide one 50'x 40' (2000 sq. ft) room to the service provider for a period not to exceed six months from the date of contract approval." (*Clear and Specific*)

In sentence #1 above, the word *adequate* can be perceived differently depending on one's perspective. For instance, the service provider may consider *adequate* to mean at least four work areas, each consisting of a minimum of 500 sq. ft. of space, whereas the client may interpret *adequate* to mean one room consisting of 100 sq. ft. Sentence #2 clearly defines the amount of workspace that the client will be providing to the service provider, as well as when and for how long the space will be made available. This is the level of detail and specificity that each SOW development team should strive to achieve.

Development and review teams often overlook ambiguities during the development and review of the SOW. Primarily focused on ensuring that all requirements for delivering a product or service are accurately captured in the document, they are less focused on and con-

To the satisfaction of the client
As determined by the client
In accordance with instructions of the client
As directed by the client
In the opinion of the client
In the judgment of the client
Unless otherwise directed by the client
To furnish if requested by the client
All reasonable requests of the client shall be complied with
Photographs shall be taken when and where directed by the client
In strict accordance with
In accordance with best commercial practice
In accordance with best modern standard practice
In accordance with best engineering practice
Workmanship shall be of the highest quality
Workmanship shall be of the highest grade
Accurate workmanship
Securely mounted

Installed in a neat and workmanlike manner
Skillfully fitted
Properly connected
Properly assembled
Good working order
Good materials
In accordance with applicable published specifications
Products of a recognized reputable manufacturer
Tests will be made unless waived
Materials shall be of the highest grade, free from defects or imperfections, and of grades approved by the client
Kinks and bends may be cause for rejection
Carefully performed
Neatly finished
Metal parts shall be cleaned before painting
Suitably housed
Smooth surfaces
Pleasing lines
Of an approved type
Of standard type

Figure 7-2. Phrases Having Multiple Meanings

cerned with the grammatical correctness of the text defining these requirements. It's often not until the project is being executed that these inconsistencies are found.

Revising the SOW to correct any ambiguities during project execution can quickly become very expensive. Sometimes the correction can be handled through a change order process; in other cases, litigation may be required to resolve the conflict. If litigation results, it won't matter what the SOW development team meant to say, what was understood, or what was spoken; it will only matter how the document reads.

To mitigate against potential ambiguities, it is extremely important that the team put itself in the position of the delivery team when reviewing the SOW. Reviewing the document from this perspective will help identify the terms or phrases that may be interpreted differently by various functional roles and organizations. It will thus be much easier for the review team to identify and correct any ambiguities prior to project execution.

2. **Don't hedge:** Hedging is the act of "hiding behind words, refusing to commit oneself or give a direct answer."[7] Individuals or teams responsible for drafting the SOW often *hedge* when:

- The requirements and expectations for the project are unclear
- They are unsure what it will take to deliver the project successfully
- An expeditious proposal response is required in a competitive bidding situation
- The project is unique or has never been done before
- The project is technically complicated or extremely risky
- They lack the skills, resources, or experience in the project being supported by the SOW.

The following is an example of a hedging type of statement.

"[Service provider] will provide a full complement of services to [client] in support of their strategic objective to become the worldwide industry leader."

The gist of this statement is that the service provider will provide any services required to assist the client in meeting its strategic objective. However, since the service provider isn't sure what services will be required to meet this objective, it is *hedging* by saying that it is going to provide all services it offers to the client. Hedging on this one single statement will immediately start a domino effect of problems for the service provider, such as:

- How to define and estimate the number and types of resources and skill sets that will be required to deliver the project
- How to price the project accurately and competitively

- How to accurately estimate the time required to deliver the product or service
- How to clearly define the success criteria for the project.

Hedging in the SOW may have short-term benefits, like helping a service provider win the work; however, it will have severe consequences when the project is being delivered. These consequences may take the form of multiple change orders, unmet service levels, and ultimately low client satisfaction ratings. These consequences may in turn lead to the demise of the project.

It is important that *hedging* not be confused with assumptions made in the document. Assumptions are data elements or factors that are considered to be true or factual and are used as part of the decision-making process; *hedging* is noncommittal and doesn't provide a baseline against which to measure change. Assumptions, on the other hand, will provide a baseline upon which change can be measured. Care should be taken to avoid terms and sentence structure that may lead to hedging in the SOW.

3. **Avoid terms of art:** "Terms of art" refers to terminology that may be specific to a particular industry or organization, but is generally not defined and understood universally. For example, a term of art commonly used by organizations performing desktop computer outsourcing services is "break-fix." This term generally refers to the repair of the hardware components making up the computer; however, unless the term is clearly defined, it could easily be misinterpreted. I'm familiar with a situation in which the SOW simply stated that the service provider would provide *break-fix* services to the client. The service provider intended this to mean that they would provide repairs to the hardware components of the client's desktop computers. The client, however, interpreted it to mean that the service provider would provide repair services to everything in the computer, including the software. Use of a term of art resulted in a lack of communication that cost the service provider tens of thousands of dollars and a tarnished reputation with the client.

It is important that the team drafting the SOW use terms that are widely recognized outside the boundaries of a particular industry or organization. If technical terms are used in the text, they must be clearly defined and understood by all parties. If any misinterpretation were to arise that resulted in legal action, the judge settling the dispute will lean toward the "ordinary and usual" meaning of the word or phrase.

4. **Avoid redundancy:** Redundancy in the SOW can reduce clarity and increase the probability of ambiguity and contradictions, which in turn may lead to claims against the party responsible for drafting the document. Claims may lead to increased costs, increased time to deliver the product or service, or both.

   If it is necessary to state the requirements in multiple sections in the SOW, then it's important that they be stated the same way in each section. Consistency is imperative. Even the slightest change in the description could lead the reader to believe that there is a new definition for the requirement, which, in turn, may result in ambiguity or outright contradiction. Paraphrasing or using synonyms to describe a requirement will also increase the potential for ambiguity in the text.

   If the requirements or specifications are spelled out in an associated document, then they may be incorporated by reference in the SOW. If revisions or exceptions are required, then specific reference should be made to the applicable portions and the change should be described.[8]

5. **Don't use nonspecific words and phrases:** Words and phrases that imply that either the service provider or the client has a choice in what is to be done or delivered should be avoided. Some of these words and phrases, along with the rationale for not using them in the SOW, are:[9]

   Any—The word "any" can be interpreted to mean an unlimited number of options. Thus, it lacks the specificity that is necessary for the SOW. Writers may use it to denote "plurality," but the reader may interpret it to mean "singularity." If the reader's interpretation is different from the writer's, it could lead to claims on the project.

   And/or—These words imply that a choice exists, and will require one of the parties identified in the SOW to make a decision about what should be used. For example, if the SOW states that "The service provider will deliver product A, B and/or C," it is not clear whether product C will actually be provided.

Assist—"Assist" is defined as the act of helping and providing aid. Its definition, however, lacks specificity regarding the range and depth of the assistance to be provided in performing the work. If this word is used, the roles and responsibilities of each party involved in the project must be clearly defined. No elements should be open for interpretation regarding who is responsible for doing what and when the work is to be completed.

As applicable/As necessary—These phrases lack clarity and are open to interpretation. The service provider's perception of what is "applicable and necessary" may be vastly different from the client's perception. The SOW must clearly define the requirements so that all parties understand what is required of them to meet their obligations.

As required—This phrase has no defined limitations and is open to interpretation by the reader. It could mean "as required" by the client, "as required" by a federal government regulation, or "as required" by an industry or organizational regulation or policy. The SOW must be specific in defining the minimum needs and limitations that must be achieved to be successful.

As directed—This phrase is similar in meaning to the word "assist" in that it refers to personal services. One party can interpret it to mean a form of supervision or oversight over another. Typically, this would refer to the service provider being directed or supervised by the client. If it is used, this phrase must clearly state what is meant by "directed" as well as who will be directing and who will be doing the work for a particular work package.

Best effort—This common phrase is frequently misused in the writing of SOWs. "Best effort" is truly in the eyes of the beholder. One person or organization may consider "best effort" to mean working 8 hours/day up to the original scheduled completion date of the project. If the project is completed within this time frame, that's great. If it's not, then the client will have to settle for the work that has been accomplished to date or approve a change order for more funding to complete the project. Another person or organization, however, may consider "best effort" to mean doing whatever it takes to get the work done on time, within budget, and of the quality desired by the client. In light of its many interpretations, this phrase should not be used in the SOW under any circumstances.

Best practice—This phrase is frequently used in writing SOWs as well as within organizations to define the best method or process for performing a task or project. However, as with the phrase "best effort," the definition of a "best practice" is in the eye of the beholder. Even within the same organization, what one may consider a best practice, another may consider antiquated. In light of the range of interpretations that may occur around this phrase, it should not be used in the SOW.

Including but not limited to—This phrase is typically used when the writer is unsure about the requirements or expectations of the project. If used in an SOW, it will create an unspecified requirement, which in turn will create ambiguity. The SOW should not contain any open-ended phrases that are subject to interpretation by the various parties.

Either—This word implies that a choice exists that will require one of the parties identified in the SOW to make a decision regarding what should be used. The SOW, however, should not contain any text that implies a choice. Instead, the text should clearly state all requirements of the work to be performed.

Etc.—Avoid using "etc." in the SOW, as it introduces unidentified, ambiguous requirements into the document. Only those known elements should be listed. Anything beyond this known list should be addressed through the change order process.

6. **Don't use catch-all and open-ended phrases:** Catch-all and open-ended phrases should be avoided in the SOW. The requirements must be specific. Avoid phrases such as "is common in the professional services industry." Such statements are vague and don't provide the reader with specifics about what is common in the professional services industry. Phrases such as "as directed" or "subject to approval" should be used only when absolutely necessary. If these phrases are used, then the performer of such actions must be clearly defined.

7. **Avoid using big words:** Writers often think they have to use big or complex words when writing an SOW. However, the focus should be on using the right word rather than a big word. This is a common problem on projects that are highly complex

or technical. The KISS (<u>K</u>eep <u>I</u>t <u>S</u>uper <u>S</u>imple) method should be applied even to these types of projects. If the document is easy to read and understand, then it's less likely to be misinterpreted or misunderstood.

8. **Avoid incorporating extraneous material and requirements:** Avoid incorporating extraneous material and data requirements that do not add value to the SOW. Only information that is essential to documenting the specific requirements of the project should be included. Extraneous information or data will add costs to the SOW without adding any value. In addition, the extraneous information may make the document vague and confusing.

9. **Avoid bias:** If the SOW is being drafted as part of a competitive bidding process, care should be taken to ensure that the document is not biased toward the products or capabilities of a particular vendor or service provider. Biased requirements may provide a vendor or service provider with a competitive advantage or disadvantage relative to other groups that may also be proposing on the work. This could lead to protests as well as lengthy delays in the procurement process. This typically applies in the government environment, but care should also be taken in the commercial sector to avoid bias in the procurement process.

10. **Avoid certain types of terminology:** Language that implies commitments for improvement, cost-reduction sharing, out-of-scope work, increasing competitiveness, and satisfying business needs should not be used in the SOW. These types of statements are difficult, if not impossible, to quantify. Something that can't be quantified should not be included in the SOW.

    Words that imply perfection like *always, never, minimum, maximum,* and *optimum* should not be used in the SOW. There is no way to ensure that something has a 100 percent chance of occurrence on a project; thus, words that imply this type of certainty should be avoided. This type of language is particularly risky for the vendor or service provider.

    The use of superlatives should also be avoided in the SOW. *All, best, every, greatest, least,* and *worst* are difficult, if not impossible, to quantify. If the statements cannot be backed up, they should not be used in the SOW.

Following these guidelines when writing an SOW will help ensure that the document is grammatically and technically sound and that it establishes a proper and solid foundation upon which to build the project. Failure to follow these guidelines, on the other hand, could ultimately lead to project failure. The benefits of taking the additional time to draft the SOW properly will far outweigh any costs incurred and will pay significant dividends later in the project.

ROLE OF THE SOW IN PRICING THE PROJECT

Before finalizing the SOW, the development team must develop a price for delivering the product or service to the client. Not only is the SOW dependent upon this price information, but the information plays a critical role in developing the SOW. Data points throughout the SOW serve as input into a pricing or cost-estimating model.

It is important to understand the distinction between *price* and *cost*. In simple terms *cost* is defined as the total amount of direct materials, direct labor, and overhead required to deliver a product or service to a client.[10] *Price* is the total cost, plus a percentage of profit margin, based on the total cost for the project. For the purpose of this discussion, the data points that serve as input into the pricing model will be referred to as pricing variables. These variables may be any quantitative data associated with a product or service being delivered to the client. For example, if a service provider were doing an IT project that called for migrating all of a clients' desktop computers from Windows 2000® to Windows XP®, then the pricing variables might include:

- Number of desktops to be migrated
- Number of locations with desktops to be migrated
- Hours available during the business day in which to perform the migration
- Number and types of resources required to perform the migration
- Universal assumptions, as well as those specific to a product or service.

For this process to work, the SOW has to be consistent with the organization's "approved" pricing model. If an organization is using multiple pricing models, then there's a very good chance that the SOW will not be consistent with any of them. This frequently happens in organizations that are decentralized, where each group is operating as a separate business unit.

It is important that a single pricing model, as well as a single model for developing SOWs, be used in the organization for this process to work properly. Although it is possible for the SOW to be customized to fit multiple

> *It is important that a single pricing model, as well as a single model for developing SOWs, be used in the organization for this process to work properly.*

pricing models, the likelihood of an organization taking the time to undertake this level of detailed effort is very low. It would also be much more cost-efficient for an organization to focus on a single model, rather than trying to apply a "one size fits all" approach.

The pricing of a project can occur at two different phases during its lifecycle. The first time is during the proposal phase. During this phase, the price will be based on the assumptions and scope captured in the PSOW. The price developed from the PSOW will be provided to the client as part of the proposal package. Ideally, if the client accepts the proposal, then the service provider will have an opportunity to perform a due diligence analysis of the client's environment to confirm that the data documented in the PSOW are valid and accurate. Based on any changes identified during the due diligence analysis, the SOW would then be revised to become the CSOW. The price for the project, in turn, would be adjusted to reflect the changes in the price variables documented in the CSOW. An example of how the price variables may be impacted between the PSOW and CSOW, for the migration project discussed earlier, is shown in Figure 7-3.

The pricing variables often become critical points of discussion during contract negotiations. Revising a pricing variable will either increase or decrease the scope of the project. If the scope changes, the price will also change. In writing the SOW, it is important that the development team is knowledgeable and experienced in:

- Understanding why and how the price is computed
- Knowing the pricing variables and the sections in which they're addressed in the SOW
- Knowing the pricing variables that have the biggest impact on the total price, as well as those that are negotiable.

Once all of the negotiations have been completed and a price has been agreed to, the price is reflected in the "pricing" section of the

Data from PSOW	Following Due Diligence	Impact on Pricing Variable
15 locations are to receive services	Another 10 locations were not originally identified, bringing the total number of locations to 25	Higher costs due to the increase in labor costs and the increase in time required to deliver the services
10,000 desktops are to be migrated	Number of desktops to be migrated increased to a total of 20,000 based on the additional 10 locations	Higher labor and software costs
Dedicated server is required to back up computers to be migrated	Server is no longer required	Lower costs since capital expenditure is no longer required
Customized reporting is required	Customized reports are not required, standard reporting will be conducted	Decrease in labor costs and software costs that would have been required to develop the custom reports

Figure 7-3. Impact of the Due Diligence Analysis on the Pricing Variables

CSOW. This then becomes the baseline price upon which all future approved changes will be based.

REVIEWING THE SOW

Once the SOW has been completed, the next step is to review the document to ensure that all requirements and obligations for delivering the product or service to the client have been properly captured. A review checklist should be developed to assist in this process. This will help ensure that nothing has been missed in the review process and also help build consistency in the way SOWs are reviewed within the organization. A sample review checklist is provided in Figure 7-4.

If time and resources are available, a peer group of subject matter experts should review the document. Ideally, this team of SMEs will mirror the make-up of the development team. If the make-up of the review team varies from that of the development team, then there is a risk that any critical element missing from the document will not be caught during the review process. If the element is significant enough, it could challenge the success of the project.

Having a separate review team is ideal, but in most cases there isn't enough time or resources available. Thus, the development team often ends up reviewing their own work. While such a review is better than none at all, the team may be so close to the content that they will overlook something that they didn't document during the original development.

It is important that the reviewers provide clear and concise comments and that their comments are referenced to specific sections in the document. Once all comments have been received, the development team can then make the appropriate revisions. A second review should be conducted to ensure that all comments have been properly addressed. The SOW is then ready to be finalized and attached as a reference in the legal contract.

ROLE OF THE SOW IN THE CONTRACT

The SOW is an integral part of the contract, sometimes referred to as the legal terms and conditions (Ts & Cs). A contract is a mutually binding agreement that obligates the service provider to provide a specified product or service and obligates the client to pay for it.[11] Contracts generally fall into one of three categories: (1) fixed price or lump sum, (2) cost reimbursable, and (3) unit price. The type of project being proposed will typically dictate the type of contract used. The SOW development team must be intimately familiar with the structure and content of the contracting form selected to ensure that nothing in the SOW duplicates or contradicts the contract.

The development team should work closely with the legal department or contracting office to ensure that the two documents are consistent and complementary. The contractual and legal implications of the SOW must also be considered during its preparation. As the project progresses, the

Checklist Item	Yes	No	If "No," provide explanation
1) Does the SOW follow the firm's approved format?			
2) Has a multidecimal or alphanumeric coding structure been used in the SOW?			
3) Is the SOW specific enough to estimate the human and nonhuman resources required to deliver the project?			
4) Did a multidisciplined TIGER team develop the SOW?			
5) Have all sections of the SOW been satisfactorily addressed?			
6) If a section of the standard SOW format didn't apply, was it marked as not applicable (N/A)?			
7) Is the SOW specific enough to price the project?			
8) Has each product or service being delivered to client been addressed in a separate subsection in the SOW?			
9) Are the requirements and obligations of both the service provider and the client clearly identifiable?			
10) Have all service levels been clearly defined and quantified?			
11) Are the deliverables to be provided and their acceptance criteria clearly defined?			
12) Have documents referenced in the SOW been properly described and cited?			
13) Have quality requirements been clearly defined to determine whether the service provider has complied with all contractual requirements?			

Figure 7-4. SOW Review Checklist (*continues*)

Checklist Item	Yes	No	If "No," provide explanation
14) Have appropriate industry standards been researched and referenced in the SOW, if necessary?			
15) Have all extraneous references and materials been eliminated?			
16) Has the SOW been checked for format and grammar?			
17) Are all supplemental data requirements referenced in the SOW and attached to the document?			
18) Has the change order process been clearly defined?			
19) Are all terms clearly defined, including "industry-wide" accepted terms?			
20) Does the SOW conflict with or contradict the language in the contract to be used?			
21) Does the review team have knowledge or experience about the type of project being supported by the SOW?			

Figure 7-4. SOW Review Checklist (continued)

service provider and the client will refer to the SOW to determine their respective rights and obligations. If a dispute arises during the delivery of the project pertaining to the performance, rights, or obligations of either the service provider or the client, the arbitrator or court will generally defer to the SOW to resolve these disputes. With the SOW taking precedence over the contract in this situation, it's imperative that the requirements and obligations of both parties be clearly defined to enhance the legal enforceability of the document. [12]

Although the SOW is part of the contract, they are two separate and unique documents. The contract addresses elements such as *force majeure*, termination clauses or penalties, employee retention clauses, confidentiality, warranties, and nonsolicitation clauses. The SOW, on the other hand, defines *what* product or service is to be provided to the client and *what* the service provider requires to deliver that product or service properly. This distinction becomes extremely important in managing changes to the project during the execution or delivery phase. If the SOW and contract were one in the same, then every time a change was proposed on a project, legal counsel would have to be involved. This would not only add unnecessary time to the review and approval process of the change order, but it would also dilute the authority of the project manager to approve changes.

To ensure segregation of the documents, the SOW should be attached to or referenced in the contract. The change order process should also address how changes will be managed on the project and clearly identify the process for managing those changes to both the contract and the SOW. A final review should be conducted prior to finalizing the contract and the CSOW to ensure that both documents are complete and do not contain any conflicts or contradictions.

Some of the guidelines discussed in this chapter are simple, commonsense steps that involve paying attention to detail. However, it is often the attention to the smallest details that pays the biggest dividends. Following these guidelines will help in drafting higher-quality SOWs for your organization. This, in turn, will lead to fewer change orders on projects, higher client satisfaction, and higher profitability.

There's a tag line from an old television commercial for oil changes that says: "You can pay me now, or you can pay me later!" This certainly holds true in SOW development. If time is dedicated to doing a quality job up front in the process, the likelihood of problems occurring later on is greatly diminished. However, if the SOW is thrown together haphazardly with little regard to details, significant problems are almost certainly going to occur later on, eventually causing the project to fail. The organization has to decide whether to do the right thing and pay the price up front, or to try and get by with as little effort as possible and pray that everything goes okay—in which case they will end up paying later. It is strongly recommended that the time be taken up front to draft the highest-quality SOW possible. It's a decision the organization won't regret.

NOTES

[1] V.A. Howard and J.H. Barton, *Thinking on Paper* (New York: William Morrow and Company, Inc., 1986).

[2] Department of Defense, *Handbook for Preparation of Statement of Work (SOW)*, MIL-HDBK-245D, 3 April 1996, p. 25.

[3] Rosemary T. Fruehling and N. B. Oldham, *Write to the Point!* (New York: McGraw-Hill, 1988).

[4] Department of Defense, p. 12.

[5] *Webster's New World Dictionary.* 2nd College Edition (New York, NY: Prentice Hall Press, 1984), p. 43.

[6] Adapted from Department of Defense, pp. 27–28.

[7] *Webster's New World Dictionary*, p. 648.

[8] NASA Handbook 5600.2A—*Statements of Work Handbook,* 23 July 1993, p. 23.

[9] Department of Defense, p. 20.

[10] Philip E. Fess and C. Rollin Niswonger. *Accounting Principles, 13th ed.* (Cincinnati, OH. South-Western Publishing Co.), 1981.

[11] J. LeRoy Ward, *Project Management Terms—A Working Glossary* (Arlington, VA: ESI International, 1997), p. 31.

[12] Department of Defense, p. 6.

Chapter 8

Sample SOWs: The Good, the Bad, and the Downright Ugly

I hear and I forget, I see and I remember, I do and I understand.

—Confucius

N ow that we've covered the foundational concepts and processes for developing an SOW, the next step is to do one! Until you actually do it yourself, you will not truly understand and appreciate what it takes to draft and implement a quality SOW on a project. The more experience you have in writing SOWs, the higher the quality of the document produced. Improving your personal and institutional proficiency at writing SOWs accrues benefits over time, particularly relating to the ultimate success of projects. Even if perfection is never achieved, the likelihood of significant oversights that may lead to project failure will be significantly reduced.

In this chapter, we will be applying the guidelines and processes discussed in Chapters 5, 6, and 7 to develop an SOW for both a complex and a simple project. The SOW for the complex project will be based on a fictitious IT outsourcing project to deliver help desk, hardware support, and software support outsourcing services to a large telecommunications organization. For the simple project, we'll be examining a sample SOW for performing a project management maturity analysis on an organization of approximately 100 employees. These examples will provide an overview of the type of information and level of detail that should go into drafting an SOW.

We will also take a look at some real-life lessons learned as they apply to selected sections within the examples. These will help identify mistakes that are commonly made when writing an SOW. We'll also identify mitigation strategies that can be applied to help avoid making the same types of mistakes.

Not only is the SOW applicable in projects of varying complexity, but it is also applicable across multiple industries. Moreover, the SOW doesn't have to be limited to our professional work projects. It can also be extremely valuable in completing personal projects. For instance, if you were working with a contractor on a home renovation project, the SOW would play a critical role in clearly defining the scope of the work to be performed, as well as the responsibilities and requirements of all parties performing work on the project. If you've ever undertaken a project like this, you know that it can be a very frustrating experience trying to get a contractor just to show up, much less to do the work the way you think it should be done. Having an SOW in place will help you consider everything you want done, as well as the way you want it done. This, in turn, will provide clarification to the contractor about what you expect on the project. You will quickly find that the project will run much smoother and at a lower cost with the SOW in place. Once you've used an SOW on one project, you will insist that one be developed for all future projects.

> *Having an SOW in place will help you consider everything you want done, as well as the way you want it done.*

COMPLEX PROJECT: GALAXY TELECOMMUNICATIONS

Galaxy Telecommunications, a large U.S.-based telecommunications company, has recently completed an internal audit of its IT capability. The audit brought to light some very disturbing issues. The results showed that the cost to provide IT services in-house was very high and that internal customer satisfaction was extremely low. Based on this information, Galaxy's Chief Information Officer (CIO) made a decision to outsource the company's weakest IT areas. As part of the solicitation process, Galaxy issued a very succinct RFP describing the types of services required to support the organization. These services included:

- Help desk services
- Hardware support services
- Software support services.

Due to the lack of resources and the ineptitude of its internal IT group, Galaxy was unable to accurately determine the current state of its technology environment. Without hard, quantifiable data available, they attempted to make assumptions regarding the state of the current environment. The following assumptions are provided in the RFP:

- 10,000 employees currently employed by Galaxy
  —5,000 employees located in the headquarters office
  —5,000 employees located in two remote locations
- Average of one computer per person (includes both desktops and laptops)
  —50% desktops
  —50% laptops
- Average of two calls/user/month coming into the help desk
- Hardware devices requiring service include computers, monitors, and printers
- Current standard software configuration made up primarily of MS® Office and several proprietary software packages
- Service levels for the various services to be proposed by the service provider and approved by Galaxy.

Galaxy requested that all responses to the RFP be turned in to its contracting department within one week from the RFP's date of issuance. Although the information provided in the RFP was at a very high level and the turnaround time was very short, APEX Consulting decided to submit a proposal to Galaxy for providing the requested services. With the short turnaround time, APEX did not have the luxury of validating the data provided in the RFP; thus, it had no choice but to accept the information as being accurate. In preparing a response to the RFP, APEX Consulting first developed a proposal SOW (PSOW) to define the scope of the services to be delivered. Being experienced in doing SOWs and delivering these types of services, APEX Consulting stated in its response that if the proposal was accepted, it would request that a period of time be allocated, prior to signing the contract, to perform a due diligence analysis of Galaxy's environment to validate the information provided in the RFP. APEX further stated that if Galaxy was unwilling to allocate time to perform this analysis, then the PSOW would act as the contract SOW (CSOW) for the project. APEX Consulting clearly communicated to Galaxy that if it was not allowed to perform a due diligence analysis, then any deviations from the information provided in the RFP would be considered changes and would be handled immediately through the change control process described in the SOW.

After reviewing the responses, Galaxy selected APEX Consulting to perform the work. Although Galaxy recognized that the data in the RFP were not as accurate as they should be, Galaxy thought they were close enough to support executing a contract. Thus, Galaxy rejected APEX Consulting's request to perform a due diligence analysis and instead opted to use the change control process to document and manage any changes from the baseline information provided in the RFP and the SOW.

The following is a sample CSOW for Galaxy's IT outsourcing project.

Contract Statement of Work

For

GALAXY TELECOMMUNICATIONS

INFORMATION TECHNOLOGY OUTSOURCING PROJECT

APEX Consulting
Atlanta, GA

TABLE OF CONTENTS

1 STATEMENT OF CONFIDENTIALITY

APEX Consulting acknowledges that the information contained in this document is confidential and proprietary to Galaxy Telecommunications. APEX Consulting agrees to use the same level of care to protect the confidentiality of this information as it uses to protect its own.

This document contains processes, techniques, and methodologies that are considered proprietary to APEX Consulting and are provided to the customer with the understanding that this information will be used for planning, executing, controlling, and closing out the project described in this document.

Each recipient of this document is expected to treat this information in the strictest confidence and is responsible for ensuring that there is no unauthorized duplication, distribution, or application of this material, unless expressly allowed in this SOW.

2 INTRODUCTION

2.1 Purpose

The purpose of this Contract Statement of Work (CSOW) is to document the services to be delivered, the price of the requested services, and the rights and responsibilities of the various parties responsible for their delivery. These services have been requested by Galaxy Telecommunications to help it meet its objective of improving the cost and quality of the information technology (IT) services being provided to its employees. This document addresses the specific requirements of Galaxy Telecommunications as well as the specific requirements of APEX Consulting to properly deliver the requested services.

Upon acceptance by both Galaxy Telecommunications and APEX Consulting, any changes or modifications to the SOW must follow the Change Control Process defined in Section 5.1 of this SOW. All approved changes will become attachments to the original approved CSOW, which will then form the new baseline upon which future changes will be measured.

> **Lessons Learned:** In some situations the client may request, or the SOW development team may decide, to title this section *Problem Statement* or *Objective Statement*. If this is the case, caution should be taken to ensure that the *problem statement* or *objective statement* is consistent with any similar statements documented in the RFP or other solicitation documents. In one case I'm familiar with, the client documented in an RFP that its objective was to double revenue and profits within three years. This objective was in turn documented in an SOW specifically for the outsourcing of a small portion of the client's IT function. It is fine for the organization to have this type of strategic objective; however, it wasn't appropriate to include it in this particular SOW. Although outsourcing some of the IT function would contribute to meeting the client's strategic objective, it was not the only factor necessary to achieve the objective. This type of statement could be understood to imply that simply outsourcing the IT function would allow the client to achieve its strategic objective of doubling revenues and profits in three years. Care should be taken not to use statements in the SOW that define objectives or problems that cannot be fully resolved by the project that the document is supporting.

2.2 Description of Work

APEX Consulting will provide an integrated IT solution to Galaxy Telecommunications, a leading global telecommunications company headquartered in Atlanta, GA, to assist Galaxy in improving the cost and quality of IT services currently being provided to its employees. This integrated solution consists of the following three (3) service offerings:

- Help Desk Services
- Hardware Support Services
- Software Support Services.

The integrated solution will be provided to Galaxy's headquarters location as well as to two remote locations in Jacksonville, Florida, and Washington, D.C. A total of 10,000 end users are currently entitled to the services noted. The distribution of these end users, by location, is as follows:

- 5,000 end users in Atlanta, GA (headquarters)
- 2,500 end users in Jacksonville, FL (remote location)
- 2,500 end users in Washington, D.C. (remote location).

Details on each of the services to be offered as part of the integrated solution are provided in Section 3.0 of this SOW.

Lessons Learned: When drafting the description of work, be sure to keep the discussion at a high level, and don't include too many specifics about the various services being offered. A detailed discussion of the services should be reserved for the section titled *Services Provided*. Also, only quantitative and qualitative information that you know to be factual should be included in this section. For example, we know from the summary of the RFP that of the 10,000 end users in the organization, 5,000 are in the headquarters office, and the remaining 5,000 are evenly distributed between the two remote locations. If an assumption has been made for a specific data element, then it needs to be addressed as either a global assumption within the Introduction section (i.e., Section 2.3 of this SOW) or as a key assumption (e.g., Section 3.1.2 of this SOW) specific to one of the service offerings being provided to the client.

2.3 Assumptions

1. Average one (1) computer per person (includes both desktops and laptops).
2. 50% of the computers are desktops, and 50% are laptops.
3. All Service Level Agreement (SLA) measurements used to measure performance will be defined by APEX Consulting and approved by Galaxy Telecommunications.
4. All SLA measurements will be calculated based on monthly averages.
5. APEX Consulting will not be held liable for any information or data lost during delivery of the requested services.
6. APEX Consulting will not be held to SLAs when delays are attributed to a manufacturer, a third-party vendor, or Galaxy Telecommunications.
7. Galaxy Telecommunications will provide all information requested by APEX Consulting to deliver the requested services properly.
8. Services can be provided to nonentitled locations on a time and materials basis; however, service to these locations will not be held to the standard SLA metrics.
9. Galaxy Telecommunications will provide a secure room in the headquarters location for storing parts and materials, which will be accessible only to APEX Consulting or Galaxy's security personnel.
10. Any hardware or software service calls received after the established hours of operation, as defined in Section 6.0, will be charged at one and a half times the standard hourly rate for calls received after hours on Monday through Friday, and twice the rate for calls received at any time on Saturday and Sunday.
11. Galaxy will provide on-site parking for all APEX Consulting personnel responding to calls outside the standard hours of operation.
12. English will be the only language used by the help desk and the hardware and software support technicians when responding to calls requesting assistance.
13. APEX Consulting will adhere to the standards of conduct as defined in Galaxy's Standard Code of Conduct.
14. Galaxy will be responsible for all costs incurred by APEX Consulting in obtaining the necessary security clearances required by Galaxy, including the cost of background checks and drug screening.
15. Non-standard hardware and software will be serviced on a time and materials basis and only after all entitled calls have been satisfactorily resolved and closed out.

16.   Galaxy Telecommunications will be responsible for providing training to APEX Consulting help desk personnel and technicians for proprietary software applications that APEX Consulting agrees to support.

> **Lessons Learned:** In most cases, very little information will be available initially for the SOW development team to use in developing the document. Thus, assumptions will have to be made to fill in the gaps of missing or outdated information. Assumptions are extremely important in the pricing of the project. If an assumption is overlooked or incorrectly stated, it could cause the total price for delivering the requested services to be drastically overestimated or underestimated. This section should document only those assumptions that are applicable to more than one service offering or those that apply universally to the project. If this example was for a PSOW, these assumptions would need to be validated during a due diligence analysis.
>
> It is strongly recommended that this section not be completed until all sections of the SOW have been completed. The development team can then easily go back and identify gaps in the information and whether some of these gaps apply to more than one service being proposed to the client. This will also help avoid redundancy in the document by ensuring that an assumption is not included as both a global assumption and an assumption specific to a particular service.

2.4 Constraints

1. Security access required at all Galaxy office locations could potentially delay the APEX Consulting personnel as well as the delivery of parts and equipment, negatively impacting APEX Consulting's ability to meet the established SLAs.
2. Pricing for the project is based on a one-year agreement, which will not allow for any reduced fee adjustments that may be gained through a long-term agreement.
3. Galaxy's internal IT group has retained control of performing all network services, including maintenance and repair of servers, hubs, and routers. Not having responsibility for all IT services could negatively impact APEX Consulting's ability to meet the agreed-to SLAs.

Lessons Learned: Constraints are included in the SOW to identify potential risks that could inhibit the service provider from delivering the requested services. Constraints can impact the price of the project, depending on the potential impact perceived by the SOW development team. If the constraint has a high probability of occurring, then additional contingencies may be included in the price of the project. The constraints may also impact the way SLAs are structured. If a constraint is significant and it has a high probability of occurring, then the development team may take a more pessimistic view of what can realistically be achieved from an SLA standpoint.

As with assumptions, this section should not be completed until all other sections of the SOW have been addressed. The development team can easily go back and identify potential constraints and determine whether they apply to more than one service being proposed to the client. This will also help to avoid redundancy in the document by ensuring that a constraint is not included as both a global constraint and a constraint specific to a particular service.

3 SERVICES PROVIDED

3.1 Help Desk Services

3.1.1 Description

APEX Consulting will provide an on-site Help Desk to support the personnel of Galaxy Telecommunications in both headquarters and remote locations. The Help Desk will be available twenty-four (24) hours a day, seven (7) days a week, except for the holidays noted in Section 6 of this SOW. It will act as the single point of contact for defining call types, tracking calls, and determining whether the incoming calls are entitled to receive the services being provided. All entitled calls will have the same level of priority and will be addressed on a first-in, first-out (FIFO) basis.

Help Desk support includes basic hardware and software troubleshooting, resolution, and dispatching of service technicians if the problem cannot be resolved by phone. APEX Consulting will only support the standard list of hardware and software approved by Galaxy Telecommunications, as defined in Sections 15.1 and 15.2 of this SOW. Any hardware or software not on these lists will not be entitled to service from APEX Consulting as part of the monthly base fee. However, upon written request from Galaxy, APEX Consulting will provide services to nonentitled hardware and software on a time and materials basis, after all entitled service calls have been satisfactorily resolved and closed out.

Based on historic call rates of 2 calls/user/month and the current number of employees entitled to services (10,000), it is estimated that 20,000 calls will be received in the Help Desk each month. Applying an abandonment rate of 5%, the total number of entitled calls/month requiring service is estimated to be 19,000. It is assumed that the number of hardware calls and software calls will be split equally. This call ratio and volume (after abandonment) will be used as the baseline factor for developing the price for delivering the Help Desk services. If the actual call volume deviates +/− 10% from this baseline factor, a change order request will be initiated in accordance with the change control process defined in Section 5.1 of this SOW.

A Help Desk Report will be developed each month and presented during the monthly project status review meeting defined in Section 5.2 of this SOW. The baseline call volume factor will also be reviewed during this meeting to determine if any deviations have occurred from the original baseline estimate.

3.1.2 Key Assumptions

1. 2 calls/user/month, with an abandonment rate of 5%.
2. Total number of entitled calls/month (after abandonment) requiring service from the Help Desk is 19,000 (baseline call volume).
3. Total call volume received by the Help Desk will be split equally between hardware and software calls.
4. APEX Consulting's Help Desk will support only the standard list of hardware components and software applications defined in Sections 15.1 and 15.2, respectively.
5. Galaxy Telecommunications will provide all required office space for the on-site Help Desk as defined in Section 7.1 of this SOW.

> **Lessons Learned:** This section should address only assumptions specific to the particular service offering. If the assumption is applicable to more than one service, then it should be captured in Section 2.3 as a global assumption. If a data element required to price the particular service accurately is not captured in the description of the service, then it should be captured as an assumption in this section.

3.1.3 Roles and Responsibilities

The roles and responsibilities of both Galaxy Telecommunications and APEX Consulting, specific to the delivery of the Help Desk service, are identified in the following matrix:

Help Desk—Roles and Responsibilities	APEX Consulting	Galaxy
1. Design and staff the on-site Help Desk.	✓	
2. Define the service level measurements.	✓	
3. Approve the service level measurements.	✓	✓
4. Provide office space for the on-site Help Desk, as defined in Section 7.1.		✓
5. Provide a list of standard hardware components and software applications entitled to service from the Help Desk.		✓
6. Produce the monthly Help Desk Report.	✓	
7. Provide training on all proprietary software requiring support.		✓

Lessons Learned: When defining the roles and responsibilities for the various services, make sure they correspond to the summary activities of the work breakdown structure (WBS) for each service. It is important not to get into the minutiae of who is responsible for every task or subtask on the project. Identifying roles and responsibilities at the summary level will provide sufficient detail.

3.1.4 Service Level Agreements (SLAs)

Help Desk SLAs	Description of SLA	Levels of Performance	Baseline Measurement Factor
Live response by the Help Desk within 60 seconds, unless the call volume exceeds more than 10% of the baseline after abandonment.	The average time it takes a member of the Help Desk staff to answer the phone and talk live with an end user. 1/	100% goal ≥ 90% acceptable < 90% unacceptable	19,000 calls/ month after 5% adandonment
1st Call Resolution –80% for the terms of the contract.	Resolution of the end user's problem on the first phone call.	100% goal ≥ 90% acceptable < 90% unacceptable 1/	19,000 calls/ month after 5% abandomnent
Unresolved calls will be escalated to a service technician within 30 minutes on a monthly average.	Assignment of calls that cannot be resolved by the Help Desk to an onsite service technician.	100% goal ≥ 90% acceptable < 90% unacceptable 1/	19,000 calls/ month after 5% abandonment

1/ The monthly average that a service level must meet to be acceptable to Galaxy Telecommunications.

These Help Desk service levels are applicable during the normal hours of operation, as defined in Section 6 of this SOW, except for the service level pertaining to the assignment of unresolved calls to a service technician. This service level will apply only during the normal hours of operation established for the hardware and software support as defined in Section 6 of this SOW. The actual service levels will be averaged on a monthly basis and reported during the regular, scheduled project review meeting.

Lessons Learned: Care should be used when defining service levels to ensure that they are specific, measurable, achievable, relevant, and time-measured. This is commonly referred to as the SMART method of defining SLAs. If the service levels cannot be measured easily, then it may be difficult to prove whether or not they are being met. From the perspective of the service provider, it is important to negotiate as long a measurement period as possible (e.g., quarterly instead of monthly). This builds in a contingency that allows the service provider two months to bring the quarterly average up to the acceptable range agreed to by both the client and the service provider. If financial penalties are tied to missed SLAs, a grace period should be allowed before the penalties take effect. Clients should also ensure that they do not require unrealistic service levels for the project, which could set the service provider up to fail. Service levels should be jointly developed and agreed to by the client and the service provider. This will ensure that both parties have had input into the measurements prior to the CSOW and the contract being finalized.

3.1.5 Deliverable(s)

The monthly Help Desk Report will address the status and performance of all services being provided to Galaxy. The report will be compiled on a monthly basis and presented to Galaxy Telecommunications during the monthly project status review meeting.

3.2 Hardware Support

3.2.1 Description

APEX Consulting will provide warranty repair services for all entitled hardware components, as defined in Section 15.2 of this SOW, at both the headquarters and remote locations of Galaxy Telecommunications. The hardware components entitled to service include printers and computers. The term *computer* is used broadly to refer to the central processing unit (CPU), monitor, keyboard, and mouse for both desktop and laptop computers. The CPU includes all internal and external components of the computer, including hard drives, floppy drives, CD players (i.e., ROM and RW), DVD ROMs, network cards, and modems. The hardware support services will be available during the normal hours of operation as defined in Section 6.0 of this SOW.

One hundred percent (100%) of the entitled hardware components are assumed to be under the Original Equipment Manufacturer (OEM) warranty. Thus, APEX Consulting will defer to the manufacturer's warranty guidelines for the process for acquiring warranty parts. It is anticipated, however, that the process will allow for a limited number of warranty parts to be stored in a secure room at the headquarters location. Repairs to printers and computers will be considered complete once the component has been restored to working order and the end user has signed off that it is working properly. If a hard drive is upgraded or replaced, APEX Consulting will be responsible only for restoring the software to the state of its last backup. Galaxy Telecommunications will be responsible for backing up any data from the hard drive prior to the upgrade or replacement. APEX Consulting will not held liable for any data lost during repairs to the hard drive.

APEX Consulting will support nonentitled hardware components on a time and materials basis, as requested by Galaxy.

3.2.2 Key Assumptions

1. Number of computers within Galaxy Telecommunications is 5,000 desktops and 5,000 laptops, as defined in Section 2.3 of this SOW.
2. Number of printers is 1,000.
3. OEM's warranty parts process will allow APEX Consulting to store a limited number of warranty parts.
4. Galaxy Telecommunications will retain responsibility for servers, hubs, routers, and all other network services not noted in this document.
5. One hundred percent (100%) of the entitled hardware components are under warranty for the life of the contract. Galaxy Telecommunications will provide proof of purchase and warranty if requested by APEX Consulting.
6. All hardware support calls will be dispatched through the on-site Help Desk. No service calls will be dispatched without coming through the Help Desk.

3.2.3 Roles and Responsibilities

Help Desk—Roles and Responsibilities	APEX Consulting	Galaxy
1. Repair or replace hardware components, as defined in Section 3.2.1, to the state of their last backup.	✓	
2. Define the hardware support service-level measurements.	✓	
3. Approve the hardware support service-level measurements.	✓	✓
4. Provide a secure room for warranty parts at the headquarters location.		✓
5. Provide a list of hardware components, including the asset tag number (if any), the name of the personnel they're assigned to, type of component, and location.		✓
6. Provide proof of purchase and warranty for all hardware components.		✓
7. Maintain a limited inventory of warranty parts on-site at the headquarters location.	✓	
8. Select and manage resources required to perform the hardware support services and meet the established service levels.	✓	

3.2.4 Service Level Agreements (SLAs)

Hardware Support SLAs	Description of SLA	Levels of Performance	Baseline Measurement Factor
Return call to requester within a monthly average of 2 hours after warranty call is placed.	The average time it takes a member of the hardware support staff to follow up with an individual requesting service for an entitled hardware component.	100% goal ≥ 90% acceptable < 90% unacceptable 1/	9,500 calls/month

continues

continued

On-site arrival within a monthly average of 8 hours after the warranty call is placed.	The average time it takes to arrive at the requester's location to analyze the problem with the hardware component.	100% goal ≥ 90% acceptable < 90% unacceptable 1/	9,500 calls/month
On-site repair within a monthly average of 16 hours after the warranty call is placed.	The average time it takes to satisfactorily repair a hardware component after the warranty call has been placed.	100% goal ≥ 90% acceptable < 90% unacceptable 1/	9,500 calls/month

1/ The monthly average that a service level must meet to be acceptable to Galaxy Telecommunications.

> **Lessons Learned:** Care must be taken in defining the service levels for hardware support because other issues outside of APEX Consulting's control may be causing the problem. For example, the key assumptions noted that Galaxy Telecommunications was retaining responsibility for servicing all servers, routers, hubs, and other network-related components. If one of these components was contributing to the hardware problem, this could impact APEX Consulting's ability to meet the established SLA. In this case, caveats should be defined in the SLAs that limit the liability of the service provider to only those things within its control. This guideline applies to any SLA that may be negatively impacted by another service provider or other third party.

3.2.5 Deliverables

Not applicable (N/A)

> **Lessons Learned:** Some sections may not require any information. In this case, there is no deliverable identified for the hardware support services. Once all reviews have been completed and the document is ready for approval, the sections tagged N/A may be deleted.

3.3 Software Support

3.3.1 Description

APEX Consulting will provide software support for installations, configurations, and troubleshooting of all standard applications, operating systems, and proprietary applications installed on Galaxy Telecommunications' computers. A list of Galaxy's software applications entitled to support services is provided in Section 15.1 (Standard Software List) of this SOW.

The on-site Help Desk will attempt to resolve any software issues over the phone; however, if the problem cannot be resolved, then it will be dispatched to a software support technician within 30 minutes. APEX Consulting's software support technicians will ensure that any software that has been installed or repaired is working and has basic functionality (defined as the ability to load the application, open and close files, make edits, and save changes). At the request of Galaxy Telecommunications, APEX Consulting will provide software support for nonstandard/nonentitled software on a time and materials basis after all entitled service calls have been satisfactorily resolved and closed out.

Galaxy Telecommunications is responsible for ensuring that all software installed on its computers has been legally obtained and properly licensed. APEX Consulting will not be responsible for, or held to, any service levels for supporting nonlicensed software that has been illegally installed on either entitled or nonentitled equipment. APEX Consulting will only install software from manufacturers that currently have agreements with Galaxy Telecommunications. APEX Consulting, in turn, will comply with the manufacturer's software licensing procedures and will not knowingly reload or restore any nonlicensed software.

APEX Consulting will use Galaxy Telecommunications' virus protection software to detect, remove, and prevent computer virus infections to computers. The software support technicians will update the virus protection software on their computers on a monthly basis. Galaxy Telecommunications will ensure that virus software has been installed on all computers. If APEX Consulting discovers that a computer does not have the proper virus protection software, a service technician will create a service ticket through the Help Desk to install the current version of virus protection. APEX Consulting will not be responsible for any damage to computers or data that may have been lost due to a virus that was not identified and eliminated by the Galaxy Telecommunications virus protection software.

Lessons Learned: APEX Consulting is signing up to support Galaxy's proprietary applications, which may be fine if APEX knows the applications and has the resources and skills required to support them. For this case study, we are assuming that APEX has this knowledge and can adequately support the software. However, if a service provider agrees to support software that it knows nothing about, this can be a huge risk to the firm's ability to meet the established service levels. In a situation like this, the SOW would need to include language requiring the client to provide the service provider with training on the proprietary software applications being used in the organization.

The only other option is to draft the SOW in such a way that it reduces or eliminates the risk to your firm, such as the service levels for the service to be provided. Be careful what you sign up for!

3.3.2 Key Assumptions

1. 9,500 software calls/month
2. All software currently existing on computers within Galaxy Telecommunications is free from viruses.
3. All software has been legally obtained and properly licensed.
4. Any software not on the standard software list in Section 15.1 of this SOW will be considered nonentitled and will not be supported by APEX Consulting.
5. Galaxy Telecommunications' virus protection software is capable of detecting and eliminating most known viruses and is updated on a monthly basis by the manufacturer.

3.3.3 Roles and Responsibilities

Help Desk—Roles and Responsibilities	APEX Consulting	Galaxy
1. Provide a list of software applications, operating systems, and proprietary applications to be supported.		✓
2. Install, configure, and troubleshoot all standard applications, operating systems, and proprietary applications, as defined in Section 15.1 of this SOW.	✓	
3. Ensure that all software that has been installed or repaired is working and has basic functionality.	✓	

continues

continued

Help Desk—Roles and Responsibilities	APEX Consulting	Galaxy
4. Ensure that all installed software has been legally obtained and properly licensed.		✓
5. Ensure that virus protection software has been installed on all computers.		✓
6. Define the software support service level measurements.	✓	
7. Approve the service level measurements for software support.	✓	✓
8. Provide a list of the software applications that make up the standard desktop/laptop configuration and are entitled to software support.		✓
9. Select and manage resources required to perform the software support services and meet the established service levels.	✓	

3.3.4 Service Level Agreements (SLAs)

Software Support SLAs	Description of SLA	Levels of Performance	Baseline Measurement Factor
Return call to requester within a monthly average of 2 hours after call is placed.	The average time it takes a member of the software support staff to follow up with an individual requesting service for an entitled software application.	100% goal ≥ 90% acceptable < 90% unacceptable 1/	9,500 calls/month
On-site arrival within a monthly average of 8 hours after the call is placed.	The average time it takes to arrive at the requester's location to analyze the problem or install a software application.	100% goal ≥ 90% acceptable < 90% unacceptable 1/	9,500 calls/month

continues

continued

On-site installation or repair within a monthly average of 16 hours after the call is placed.	The average time it takes to install or repair a software application to where it is providing basic functionality.	100% goal ≥ 90% acceptable < 90% unacceptable <u>1/</u>	9,500 calls/month

<u>1/</u> The monthly average that a service level must meet to be acceptable to Galaxy Telecommunications.

3.3.5 Deliverables

N/A

4 GENERAL ROLES AND RESPONSIBILITIES

4.1 Corporate Responsibilities

4.1.1 Galaxy Telecommunications

- Galaxy will provide the necessary access to headquarters and remote locations, including security access, employee/visitor badges, network ID cards, secure room keys, and parking passes.
- Galaxy will provide all information and access to knowledge holders required for APEX Consulting to fully define the scope of the work described in this SOW.
- Galaxy's employees will be responsible for performing all data backup activities prior to service being performed by APEX Consulting.
- Galaxy will coordinate all services being provided within the organization, including those being performed by other vendors or internal groups, to ensure that there is no duplication of effort or negative impact to APEX Consulting's ability to meet the established service levels.
- Galaxy will approve the service levels defined by APEX Consulting.

4.1.2 APEX Consulting

- APEX Consulting will provide Help Desk, hardware support, and software support services, including any deliverables defined in this document, within the mutually agreed-upon time frame defined in Section 11 of this SOW.
- APEX Consulting will comply with the standards of conduct defined in both Galaxy's and APEX Consulting's Standard Code of Conduct.
- APEX Consulting will be responsible for the selection and management of the personnel required to achieve the established service levels.

4.2 Executive Steering Committee

The Executive Steering Committee (ESC) will comprise senior executives from both Galaxy Telecommunications and APEX Consulting and will meet on a quarterly basis, as defined in Section 5.2 of this SOW. APEX Consulting's project manager will be responsible for scheduling and coordinating the logistics for the quarterly meetings. The ESC's responsibilities include:

- Evaluating APEX Consulting's performance in delivering the services
- Resolving issues that require the ESC's review, guidance, or approval
- Establishing both strategic and tactical continuous improvement objectives.

The ESC will consist of the following representatives from Galaxy Telecommunications and APEX Consulting:

Galaxy Telecommunications

- Chief Information Officer (CIO)
- Director of Information Technology
- Director of Procurement

APEX Consulting

- Senior Vice President of Services
- Regional Director of Services
- Regional Sales Manager

Lessons Learned: At the discretion of the development team or the client, this section may include profiles or functional descriptions for each of the functional team members required to deliver the requested services. These profiles or descriptions generally do not add value or benefits to the SOW, other than providing a high-level list of the functional skill sets required for the services. One of the most common mistakes made when documenting the roles and responsibilities is to identify specific individuals for the various functional roles. In most cases, this is done at the request of the client.

Even if a specific individual is identified in the SOW, it doesn't guarantee that they will be with the project from initiation through completion. Defining the roles and responsibilities down to this level of detail should be avoided if at all possible. It is acceptable, however, to list the various functional roles and descriptions. Rather than focusing on *who* is delivering it, the emphasis should be on *what* is being delivered. Doing this places the responsibility on the service provider to ensure that it pulls together the most capable and qualified team available to meet the established service levels or product requirements. Again, the service levels are not measuring the performance of individuals, but rather that of the team as a whole.

Another advantage of addressing only the functional roles or skill sets is that if there is a change to a member of the team, then a change order will not have to be processed to document the change in the SOW. If a specific individual is identified in the SOW and he or she is replaced midway through the project, this would be considered a change to the SOW and project,

continues

continued

thus requiring a change order. This can be a very time-consuming process that can cause unnecessary delays to the overall project completion date.

The detailed level should be reserved for the project management documents, which do not carry a contractual obligation. Then if a change occurs, the service provider will not be contractually obligated to have a specific individual on the team; its only obligation will be to meet the established service levels with the resources available at that time. If it can't meet the service levels, it will likely incur a financial penalty. Again, this puts the responsibility on the service provider to put the best team forward to deliver the services successfully and meet the established service levels.

5.1 Change Control Process

A Change Order Request Form must be completed for all changes, requested by either APEX Consulting or Galaxy Telecommunications, that impact or deviate from the approved SOW. The APEX Consulting Project Manager will be responsible for managing all change order requests submitted on the project in accordance with the following process:

1. All change order requests must be submitted in writing to the APEX Project Manager, either by e-mail or hard copy, to be recognized as a formal request. Verbal requests or voice mails will not be considered formal change order requests. The Change Order Request Form, shown in Section 15.5 of this SOW, should be used to document in detail the change and justification for why it is needed. The initial submission must also document the estimated work effort and cost specifically for implementing the change if approved. If APEX Consulting conducts an investigation for any change requests submitted by Galaxy Telecommunications, then the cost to perform this investigation will be billed to Galaxy on a time and materials basis (unless otherwise noted or agreed to).

2. Based on the estimated work effort and cost, representatives from both Galaxy and APEX will jointly determine whether to proceed with the investigation. The approval levels established for both Galaxy Telecommunications and APEX Consulting are as follows:

APEX Consulting—Approval Limits

Title:	Changes Up to:
Project Manager	$50,000
Regional Director of Services	$100,000
Senior VP of Services	Over $100,000

Galaxy Telecommunications—Approval Limits

Title:	Changes Up to:
Program Manager	$25,000
Director of Information Technology	$50,000
Chief Information Officer (CIO)	Over $50,000

If the investigation is rejected, then the change order request is considered rejected and no further action is required. If it is accepted, then the requester (or the requester's assignees) will determine the impact of implementing the change on the project.

3. In investigating the impact of the change on the project, the requester (or the requester's assignees) will determine the impact on the cost, schedule, and manpower originally estimated for the project. They will also determine the impact on the SOW and any revisions to the language that may be required, as well as the estimated work effort and cost to implement the change. Once the investigation has been completed, the requester will complete the Change Order Request Form with the information gathered in this step and resubmit it to the project manager for coordinating the review and approval.

4. Based on the estimated work effort and cost, representatives from Galaxy and APEX will jointly determine whether to proceed with implementing the change. The approval levels required for both Galaxy Telecommunications and APEX Consulting are shown in step 2 above. If the implementation is rejected, then the change order request is considered rejected and no further action is required. If the implementation is accepted, the change order request is considered approved. Once all the appropriate signatures have been obtained, the approved change order will then be attached, as an amendment, to the SOW. The amended SOW will become the new baseline document.

5.2 Meetings

Galaxy Telecommunications and APEX Consulting will jointly participate in various meetings to review the progress of the project. The following table identifies the type of meeting, the frequency, and the proposed attendees.

Type of Meeting	Frequency	Galaxy Attendees	APEX Consulting Attendees
Project Review Meeting	Monthly (First Tuesday of every month)	Program Manager/ Director of Information Technology	Project Manager/ Regional Director of Services
Weekly Status Meeting	Every Tuesday from 9:00 a.m.– 11:00 a.m.	Program Manager	Project Manager/ Team Leads (as necessary)
Executive Steering Committee Meeting	Quarterly	CIO/Director of Information Technology/ Director of Procurement	Sr. VP of Services/ Regional Director of Services/ Regional Sales Manager

5.3 Billing Process

The billing process for this engagement is as follows:

- APEX Consulting will invoice Galaxy Telecommunications monthly, in advance, for entitled fixed price services. Invoices will be submitted to Galaxy's Accounts Payable in electronic or paper form on the last day of the prior month.
- Time and materials based services provided by APEX Consulting will be invoiced to Galaxy Telecommunications as incurred in arrears.
- Travel and other related expenses will be invoiced as defined in Section 12.5 of this SOW.
- Galaxy's accounts payable representative(s) will process the checks for the services rendered and will mail them to APEX Consulting's headquarters office in Atlanta, GA.
- Invoices will be paid on a net thirty (30) basis. Galaxy will pay a one (1) percent per month charge on all past due invoices.

Lessons Learned: Documenting the billing process may seem trivial, but it can make a big difference in the execution and delivery of services. In one case I'm familiar with, the service provider didn't take the time to document properly how the services were going to be billed to the client. When it came time to issue the first bill, no one was sure where to send the bill or how long the client had to pay it. The confusion led to a significant delay in receiving payment from the client. It also delayed the delivery of some of the services being provided to the client, which in turn meant that the team was unable to meet the established service levels.

5.4 Dispute Resolution

Any disputes that may arise between Galaxy Telecommunications and APEX Consulting during the delivery of the requested services will be addressed through the following process:

Step 1: All issues or disputes that cannot be resolved by those involved should be escalated to APEX Consulting's project manager and Galaxy's program manager.

Step 2: If the parties identified in step 1 cannot resolve the issue or dispute, then it should be escalated to APEX Consulting's Regional Director of Services and Galaxy's Director of Information Technology.

Step 3: If the parties identified in step 2 cannot resolve the issue or dispute, then it should be escalated to APEX Consulting's Senior Vice President of Services and Galaxy's Chief Information Officer (CIO).

Step 4: If the parties identified in step 3 cannot resolve the issue or dispute, then an independent party will be brought in to mediate and arbitrate the resolution of the issue or dispute.

Step 5: If the independent arbitrator fails to reach a resolution, then the parties may choose to proceed to litigation. This is the least desirable option, and it should be avoided if at all possible.

5.5 Reports

APEX Consulting will be responsible for producing reports as scheduled below. APEX Consulting will produce customized or ad hoc reports only upon written request from Galaxy Telecommunications. The time required to design and develop the customized or ad hoc reports will be charged to Galaxy Telecommunications on a time and materials basis.

Report Type	Frequency
Help Desk Report	Monthly
SLA Compliance Report	Monthly

Lessons Learned: Service providers often make the mistake of agreeing to produce an entire portfolio of reports for the client without really knowing how much effort will be required—not only to design and develop the reports, but also to gather the data needed to complete them. Before agreeing to produce a report or deliverable in the SOW, care should be taken to ensure that it can actually be done. If it is determined that a certain report or deliverable cannot be produced after the SOW has been executed, then the service provider will be liable for the costs to design, develop, and produce the report. It could also negatively impact any SLAs that may be tied to the report, which in turn could lead to a financial loss for the service provider.

If the client requests a customized report after the SOW has been executed, then the service provider should charge the client for the time to design, develop, and produce the report. Service providers will often do this as a courtesy and not charge the client for the effort. However, be aware that more is involved than just the design and development time. This report will have to be generated each reporting period, which means that resources will have to be dedicated to gathering data and producing the report. This can equate to a significant sum of money over time and can ultimately reduce overall gross profit for the project.

6 HOURS OF OPERATION

The standard hours of operation for services being provided to Galaxy Tele-communications are from 8:00 a.m. to 5:00 p.m. Eastern Standard Time (EST), Monday through Friday, at both the headquarters and the remote locations. This also defines the standard business day for APEX Consulting. The hours of operation for each of the APEX Consulting services identified in this SOW are as follows:

Service	Standard Hours of Operation	After Hours Support
Help Desk	24 hours/7days (except for the holidays noted below)	N/A
Hardware Support	8:00 a.m.–5:00 p.m. EST, Monday thru Friday	Support will be provided for standard hardware components entitled for service. (SLAs will not apply.)
Software Support	8:00 a.m.–5:00 p.m. EST, Monday thru Friday	Support will be provided for standard software applications entitled for service. (SLAs will not apply.)

APEX Consulting will observe all Galaxy Telecommunications holidays listed below. Galaxy will be responsible for notifying APEX Consulting, in writing, 60 days prior to the start of each calendar year, of the dates on which each of these holidays will be observed.

- New Year's Day
- Martin Luther King Day
- Presidents Day
- Memorial Day
- Independence Day
- Labor Day
- Veterans Day
- Thanksgiving Day and the day after
- Christmas Day.

If any of the Galaxy Telecommunications locations are closed for any reason, such as weather, health concerns, safety, or special events, then APEX Consulting will be relieved of its obligation to meet the affected SLAs. Galaxy Telecommunications will also be responsible for reimbursing APEX Consulting for any costs or expenses incurred due to an unscheduled closing.

7 FACILITIES/TOOLS/EQUIPMENT REQUIREMENTS

The following are the minimum facility requirements for APEX Consulting to deliver the services identified in this SOW properly. Galaxy Telecommunications will be responsible for ensuring that these facilities are provided to APEX Consulting prior to work being initiated and that the facilities will be at least equivalent to those provided to Galaxy's own employees. Galaxy will also be responsible for all costs associated with the acquisition and use of the facilities, including all charges for the installation and use of phones and modem lines. All facilities provided to APEX Consulting must meet the minimum handicap requirements as defined by the Americans with Disabilities Act of 1990 and the Occupational Safety and Health Act of 1970. Failure to meet these minimum facility requirements will inhibit APEX Consulting's ability to meet the established SLAs and will prohibit Galaxy Telecommunications from enforcing any financial penalties for missed SLAs.

Facilities provided to APEX Consulting will be accessible only to its employees and authorized Galaxy personnel. The facilities will be fitted with locks, card key entry, and/or electronic security pads. Galaxy Telecommunications will also provide APEX Consulting with access to conference rooms, cafeterias, parking, health club facilities, and other similar facilities at no charge or at a charge commensurate with that charged to Galaxy's own employees.

The following facilities and equipment are required by APEX Consulting to perform the requested services properly (no specific tools are required):

Facility/Tool/Equipment	Description	Location
Management Office Space	One enclosed office for each manager or team lead. Minimum of 100 sq. ft. per office. Office to include, at a minimum, a desk, chair, trashcan, lights (desk and overhead), two visitor chairs, and two 3-drawer filing cabinets.	• Headquarters and remote locations
Help Desk Office Space	A separate cubicle, minimum of 64 sq. ft. per cubicle, for each Help Desk staff member and hardware and software service technician. Cubicle to include, at a minimum, a desk, chair, trashcan, desk light, and 3-drawer filing cabinet.	• Headquarters

continues

continued

Hardware and Software Support Services Office Space	10 cubicles, with a minimum work area of 64 sq. ft., to be shared by hardware and software support technicians. 10 cubicles will be required at each Galaxy location, for a total of 30 cubicles. Cubicle to include, at a minimum, a desk, chair, trashcan, desk light, and one mobile 3-drawer filing cabinet for each support technician using the space.	• Headquarters and remote locations
Analog Data Lines	Minimum of one modem line for each enclosed office and cubicle provided.	• Headquarters and remote locations
Telephone Lines w/ Phones	Minimum of one phone line with phone for each enclosed office and cubicle provided.	• Headquarters and remote locations
Secure Storage Room	Secure room, with a minimum working area of 300 sq. ft. (20'x15') for storing parts and materials. Only APEX Consulting staff and Galaxy security personnel will have access.	• Headquarters
Fax Machines	Minimum of one fax machine for each location.	• Headquarters and remote locations
Printers	Minimum of one laser jet printer (or equivalent) for every 10 employees.	• Headquarters and remote locations
Copy Machines	Minimum of one copy machine for each location.	• Headquarters and remote locations
Work Benches (w/power strips)	One 4'x 10' workbench, with power strips, for each location's service support office space.	• Headquarters and remote locations
HVAC	Heating and air conditioning available and working in all work areas being provided.	• Headquarters and remote locations
Lights and Temperature Control	Lights and temperature control available and working in all work areas being provided.	• Headquarters and remote locations

Lessons Learned: Documenting the facilities, equipment, and tools required to deliver services properly to a client is commonly overlooked by service providers. However, it can play a critical role in determining the success of the project. When identifying the facility requirements, it is important to be very specific and detailed. In fact, in some situations it may even be necessary to identify the need for trashcans and coat racks. This may seem trivial, but I've talked with service delivery teams that became so frustrated at the lack of a coat rack for the team that morale declined to the point where they were trying to get transferred to a new project. The poor morale was also contributing to a decline in their performance and failure to meet the established service levels. In this particular situation, it was wintertime and the team was working in very close quarters with very little free space. They were forced to lay their coats on the floor, which was not only inconvenient, but it was also a safety hazard for anyone trying to walk around the room. After several weeks of escalating this issue, they were finally provided a coat rack. This one simple item made a tremendous difference in their attitude and their performance.

One of the requirements is that all facilities being provided to APEX Consulting must, at a minimum, meet the handicap requirements as defined by the Americans with Disabilities Act of 1990 and the Occupational Safety and Health Act of 1970. In some cases this particular statement may be captured in the legal terms and conditions; if it isn't, then it must be captured in this section. In another real-life example that illustrates the importance of this statement, a service provider providing hardware support services for a very large organization had properly documented in the SOW the need for a large work area for servicing the hardware components. What they didn't do was to document that the area needed to be easily accessible for those team members who were handicapped. As it turned out, the client provided them with a workspace in the basement of its main office, which was only accessible by a dumb waiter and a staircase several stories high. Since the handicapped team members were unable to get to the workspace, they were forced to work in a separate area, which ended up being a converted storage closet. The space was so limited that only one or two people could work in the area at one time. The limited space also did not allow them to store the necessary tools to perform their work; thus, they started missing the established service levels. This, in turn, led to financial penalties against the service provider simply because the workspace provided was not accessible by all of the service technicians. Attention to the little details like this can make the difference between a successful project and a failed project.

8 SERVICE RESPONSIBILITY TRANSFER

Galaxy Telecommunications will be responsible for closing out all hardware and software service calls received up to the start date of services being delivered by APEX Consulting. After this date, APEX Consulting will be responsible for all hardware and software calls coming into the on-site Help Desk. APEX Consulting will address any outstanding hardware or software calls only after written request by Galaxy Telecommunications. The cost for addressing these outstanding calls will be billed to Galaxy on a time and materials basis.

Lessons Learned: If an incumbent third-party vendor or internal client group is being replaced, it must be clear when and where its responsibility ends and where the new service provider's responsibility starts up. One service provider I know was awarded a project to implement an on-site help desk for a client, which was replacing a help desk being run by another outside vendor. The SOW did not include any language specifically delineating when the incumbent vendor's responsibility ended and when the new service provider's responsibility started. The new service provider ended up inheriting a significant number of backlogged calls from the old provider, which caused the new provider to fall behind immediately in meeting the established service levels; as a result, it faced financial penalties after the first month of service. Fortunately, the client understood the situation and allowed the service provider to negotiate a separate arrangement for handling the backlogged calls. If the client had not been as understanding, the service provider could have incurred significant financial losses .

9 SECURITY REQUIREMENTS

9.1 Facilities

Galaxy Telecommunications will provide APEX Consulting a list of all facilities and areas within those facilities that require security access for their employees to perform the services. The list will also address the type of security access required for each area identified.

9.2 Personnel

Galaxy Telecommunications will provide security access to APEX Consulting personnel for all appropriate areas within five (5) business days of the assigned start date. If security clearance is not provided within the five (5) business days, Galaxy Telecommunications will provide an escort to the service technicians providing service in the secure areas. If APEX Consulting is unable to meet the established service levels due to the lack of security access or an escort, no financial penalties will be imposed. APEX Consulting will not be held to any SLAs until all security access requirements have been met by Galaxy Telecommunications. Galaxy will cover all costs associated with obtaining the security clearances, including background checks, drug screening, and any other checks or tests required.

Lessons Learned: The failure to document properly the facilities or areas within a client's organization that require security access, and the type of access required, can contribute to a service provider not meeting the established service levels.

In one case, the service provider was awarded a contract to provide desktop support services to a large energy company, which also included nuclear power facilities. In negotiating the SOW and associated service levels, no one took into consideration the need for the service technicians to have security access. Thus, when the first service call came in that required a technician to be dispatched to the nuclear facility, the technician was unable to get in because of lack of appropriate security access. The service provider immediately started incurring financial penalties for not meeting the service levels. It also had to pay for all background checks and drug screening required by the client to obtain the security clearance for all of its employees. These costs and penalties could easily have been avoided if time had been taken initially to document these requirements properly during initial development of the SOW.

---

10 MARKETING REQUIREMENTS

10.1 Marketing Plan

APEX Consulting and Galaxy Telecommunications will jointly develop an internal marketing plan to inform Galaxy's employees of the IT services being made available. The plan will address various methods of communicating with Galaxy's employees to make them aware of what services are available and how to go about requesting assistance from APEX Consulting. The methods of communication may include mouse pads, firmwide e-mail announcements, company newsletters, lunch and learn sessions, and individual flyers. This plan will be completed within five (5) business days after the start of services.

Galaxy Telecommunications will be responsible for all costs associated with the design, development, and deployment of the marketing materials in all Galaxy locations.

> **Lessons Learned:** Marketing requirements may not be applicable for every type of project; however, in situations where a group of people need to be informed of a service or product being provided, consider including a marketing section in the SOW. Otherwise both the client and the service provider will likely incur unexpected costs.
>
> As noted in Chapter 6, a sales manager on one project I'm familiar with promised the client that the service provider would provide all employees with a mouse pad announcing a new service being offered. However, neither the sales manager nor the client budgeted for this expense. Although the promise might have seemed trivial at the time, the expense was significant—to the tune of $90,000. Since the sales manager for the service provider had made the commitment, the service provider ended up absorbing the cost.

11 SCHEDULE

The following table identifies the completion dates of the major milestones that were identified in the initial schedule for delivering IT outsourcing services to Galaxy Telecommunications. Upon approval of the CSOW and the contract, these dates will become the baseline schedule upon which future changes will be measured.

Major Milestone	Completion Date
Contract and CSOW approved	1 June 20XX
Planning Completed	1 July 20XX
Implementation of Services Completed	1 August 20XX
Steady-State Operations Achieved[1]	1 October 20XX
Project Complete[2]	1 June 20XX (one year later)

1. Since this is an outsourcing project, once steady-state operations are achieved, the project will move into a maintenance phase for the remainder of the contract.
2. The IT outsourcing project with Galaxy Telecommunications is a one-year agreement, with the start date being the execution date of the contract and the CSOW.

Lessons Learned: When documenting schedule dates in this section of the SOW, keep the discussion at a high level and don't get into the details of the full schedule. Only the major milestones and their associated completion dates should be included. (The full schedule may be included as an attachment to the SOW.) It is also important to note that the scheduled dates do not become the baseline dates until both the client and the service provider have approved the contract and the supporting CSOW.

12 PRICING

12.1 Service Pricing Assumptions

Pricing for the services being provided to Galaxy Telecommunications is based on the following data and assumptions documented throughout this SOW:

1. One-year agreement.
2. 10,000 end users entitled to services.
3. One (1) computer per person.
4. 5,000 desktops and 5,000 laptops.
5. Total 1,000 printers split proportionately among the three Galaxy locations.
6. Two (2) calls/user/month with a 5% abandonment rate for a total 19,000 calls/month into the Help Desk. If the call volume exceeds +/− 10% of the baseline, a change request will be initiated.
7. Total call volume per month will be equally split between hardware (9,500) and software (9,500) calls.
8. Services can be provided to nonentitled locations on a time and materials basis; however, service to these locations will not be held to the standard SLA metrics.
9. Any service calls, regardless of type, received after the established hours of operation, as defined in Section 6.0 of this SOW, will be charged at one and a half times the standard hourly rate for calls received after hours on Monday through Friday, and twice the rate for calls received at any time on Saturday and Sunday.
10. Nonstandard hardware and software will be serviced on a time and materials basis and only after all entitled calls have been satisfactorily resolved and closed out.
11. One hundred percent (100%) of entitled hardware components are under warranty for the life of the project.

Pricing for the delivery of the requested services is structured into the following categories: ramp-up or one-time fees, base monthly fees, time and material rates, travel and expenses, shipping fees, and termination fees.

> **Lessons Learned:** The pricing section can be addressed in many different ways, from stating a single price for the delivery of a product to an à la carte pricing structure for every type of service being provided. Using an à la carte pricing structure adds a great deal complexity to drafting the SOW. The more factors that are introduced into the billing process, the greater the chance of inconsistencies or redundancies occurring, possibly leading to errors and confusion in the accounting process. Keeping the pricing structure simple will help the client understand the price it is being charged for the product or service it is receiving. This will decrease the likelihood of the fees being challenged. It will also help the service provider in its billing process by ensuring that all products or services being provided to a client are billed properly and that no money is being left on the table.

12.2 Ramp-up Fees

A one-time ramp fee of $250,000 will be charged to cover the costs associated with the following items:

- Development of processes and procedures
- Training manuals and courses
- Recruiting and staffing
- Relocation of resources
- Travel.

12.3 Base Monthly Fees

A base fee of $200/computer/month will be billed for the services identified in Section 3 of this SOW (*Services Provided*).

If the number of entitled computers changes by +/– 10% from the baseline number of 10,000, then a change order request will be initiated to revise the price of the services being delivered. Similarly, a change order request to adjust the price will be initiated if the call volume changes by +/– 10%.

12.4 Time and Materials

All time and materials services identified in this SOW will be billed at the rates shown in the table below. This includes hardware and software support services provided after standard business hours, as well as services provided for nonentitled hardware components and software applications as identified in the SOW. APEX Consulting will also assist Galaxy Telecommunications with special projects on a time and materials basis, provided that sufficient resources are available to meet the request.

APEX Consulting Functional Role	Hourly Rate
Software Support Technician	$90.00
Hardware Support Technician	$90.00
Project Manager	$150.00

12.5 Travel and Expenses

APEX Consulting will bill Galaxy Telecommunications for all travel-related expenses when an APEX employee is required to travel to provide services. Travel expenses will be reimbursed by Galaxy Telecommunications as follows:

- $0.36 per mile when using personal auto
- $150/day per diem (covers lodging and meals)
- Actual cost of other travel-related expenses, plus a 9% service charge. This includes expenses for phone calls, taxis, rental cars, dry cleaning, and airfares.

12.6 Shipping Fees

If APEX Consulting is required to use an overnight or express delivery service to meet the established service levels, the cost for such services will be billed to Galaxy Telecommunications as incurred. APEX Consulting will use Galaxy's preferred delivery vendor for the shipping services.

12.7 Termination Fees

If Galaxy Telecommunications terminates the contract without cause or for convenience, the termination fees will be equivalent to a total of three (3) months' worth of billing for base services of 10,000 computers or the total number of computers entitled to services at the time of termination.

12.8 Penalties and Bonuses

For all services identified in this SOW, APEX Consulting must meet the established service level at least 90% of the time during the measurement period for Galaxy Telecommunications to consider the services to be acceptable. If APEX Consulting does not meet this 90% compliance level, then a financial penalty will be imposed. The penalty may be deducted from the total monthly base fees billed to Galaxy. The lower the percentage of compliance, the greater the financial penalty. The maximum penalty imposed will not exceed 1.5%. If the service level compliance is 95% or greater, Galaxy will pay a 1.0% bonus to APEX Consulting. The percentages used to determine the penalties and bonuses will be computed as a percentage of the total monthly base fees billed to Galaxy. The percentages to be applied are shown in the table below:

Percentage of SLA Compliance	Percentage of Penalty and Bonus
79.9% or less	−1.50%
80%–84.9%	−1.25%
85%–89.9%	−1.0%
90%–94.9%	0%
95% or greater	1.0%

13 SIGNATURE BLOCK

APEX Consulting   **Galaxy Telecommunications**

_____   _____

Date:_____   Date:_____
Senior VP of Services   Chief Information Officer

_____   _____

Date:_____   Date:_____
Regional Director of Services   Director of Information Technology

_____   _____

Date:_____   Date:_____
Regional Director of Sales   Director of Procurement

_____   _____

Date:_____   Date:_____
Project Manager   Program Manager

Lessons Learned: The purpose of this section is to ensure that both the service provider and the client agree to the scope of the services being provided and that the requirements of both parties have been adequately addressed. Since the SOW is a supporting document to the legal terms and conditions, some organizations may choose to delete this section and simply use the signature section of the contract to confirm acceptance of the SOW. However, if an umbrella agreement or master services agreement is in place between a client and a service provider, then it is strongly recommended that this approval section be included in the SOW. When an umbrella or master services agreement is in place, multiple SOWs will often be developed under one agreement. In this situation, the SOWs may have various project sponsors and executives responsible for their success; thus, it is important that there be a signature section showing their concurrence and acceptance of the scope of the project to be delivered.

14 GLOSSARY OF TERMS

Term	Definition
Application	A business productivity software tool, which can be an off-the-shelf "shrink wrapped" product, a customized off-the-shelf product, or a proprietary software tool developed internally.
Average Call-Back Time	Average amount of time it takes the Help Desk or support technician to return a call from an entitled end user requesting assistance.
Backup	The function of copying or archiving data files from a computer to a floppy disk, compact disc (CD), or tape drive to ensure the recovery of information that may be lost during the delivery of services.
Basic Functionality	The ability to load an application, open and close files, make edits, and save changes.
Central Processing Unit	All internal and external components of the computer, including hard drives, floppy drives, CD players (i.e., ROM and RW), DVD ROMs, network cards, and modems.
Desktop	A personal computer consisting of a central processing unit (CPU), monitor, keyboard, and mouse.
Entitled	Computers or end users that may receive the services being provided.
Escalation Process	A management process in which the priority of a service request is revised based on the difficulty of achieving resolution or the impact of the request on meeting the established service levels.
In Scope	Services defined in Section 3 of this SOW.
Laptop	A personal computer that contains a CPU, monitor, keyboard, and mouse within a single unit, and is small enough to be used as a mobile unit in multiple locations.

Out of Scope	Products or services not specifically defined in this SOW.
Personal Computer (PC)	See *Desktop* or *Laptop*.
Project	The delivery of services with a clearly defined start and end date and supported by a single SOW.
Resolution Time	The total amount of time involved in resolving a caller's problem.
Service Level	A quantifiable benchmark established to measure performance of a service being provided to the client.
Service Level Agreement (SLA)	Legally binding service level objectives for each service, mutually agreed to by the client and the service provider, that establish specific and measurable levels of performance that the client considers to be acceptable and that the service provider can realistically deliver.
Shrink-wrap	Commercially available software applications that may be considered part of the standard software image on the client's computers.
SOW	Statement of work.
Standard	A mutually agreed-upon list of hardware components and software applications that the service provider will be responsible for servicing under the contract.
Statement of Work	A narrative description of the products and services to be supplied to the client and the needs and requirements of the contractor to deliver such products and services properly under the contract.

15 ATTACHMENTS

15.1 Standard Software Application List

Application	Versions Supported
Microsoft® (MS) Windows	95 and 2000
Microsoft® XP	
MS® Word	95 and 2000
MS® Excel	95 and 2000
MS® Access	95 and 2000
MS® PowerPoint	95 and 2000
Microsoft® Outlook	2000
Microsoft® Project	98 and 2000
Galaxy Accounting Software	Proprietary software
AMCE Resource Management Software	Proprietary software
Norton Antivirus®	Latest release

15.2 Standard Hardware Component List

Hardware components entitled to service from APEX Consulting include all desktops, laptops, and printers that have a Galaxy Telecommunications asset tag. APEX Consulting will support nonentitled hardware components (i.e., hardware components not having a Galaxy Telecommunications asset tag) on a time and materials basis, as requested by Galaxy.

15.3 Customer Site Listing

Galaxy Telecommunications Office	Location
Headquarters	Xxxx Peachtree Street, N.E. Atlanta, Georgia xxxxx
Northeast Regional Office	Xxxx Wisconsin Ave. Washington, D.C. xxxxx
Southeast Regional Office	Xxxx Baymeadows Road Jacksonville, Florida xxxxx

15.4 Change Order Request Form

CHANGE ORDER REQUEST FORM			Change Order No.
SECTION 1 - PROJECT INFORMATION			
Client Name:		Project Name:	
Project Manager:		Project Number:	
PM's Phone Number:			
SECTION 2 - CHANGE REQUEST INFORMATION			
Initiated by:		Date Submitted:	
Initiator's Phone Number:		Date Completed:	
Description of Change Request:			
Justification for Change Request:			
SECTION 3 - CHANGE REQUEST INVESTIGATION DECISION			
Estimated Work Effort to Investigate:		Actual Work Effort to Investigate:	
Estimated Cost to Investigate:		Actual Cost to Investigate:	
☐ Investigation Accepted	Client Representative(s):		Date:
☐ Investigation Rejected	Service Provider Representative(s):		Date:
Reason for Rejection:			
SECTION 4 - CHANGE REQUEST IMPLEMENTATION DECISION			
Impact of Change Request on SOW			
SOW Section	Impact/Change		
Category of Change	From	To	
Cost			
Schedule			
Manpower			
Estimated Work Effort to Implement:		Actual Work Effort to Implement:	
Estimated Cost to Implement:		Actual Cost to Implement:	
☐ Implementation Accepted	Client Representative(s):		Date:
☐ Implementation Rejected	Service Provider Representative(s):		Date:

15.5 Sample Reports

15.5.1 Help Desk Report

[The customized Help Desk Report for this IT outsourcing project should be inserted here, along with any additional reports that are required as part of this project.]

15.5.2 SLA Compliance Report

[The customized SLA Compliance Report for this IT outsourcing project should be inserted here.]

SIMPLE PROJECT: COMPANY USA

Not every SOW has to be 60, 80, or 100 pages long. For projects that are not as complex or are smaller in scope, the SOW may be more succinct and require less detail. This does not mean, however, that the SOW is less important for smaller projects than it is for their larger counterparts. In fact, the SOW may be even more important for simple projects.

Often, if a project is thought to be simple or is small in scope, the perception is that there's no need to do a detailed SOW. This is particularly true if an organization has experience doing a certain type of project. The organization has done this type of work before, so why waste time and resources drafting a document to define the scope of work when they can simply tell the client what they're going to do, sign the contract, execute the work, and collect their fees? It's this type of arrogance and lack of attention to detail that can cause even the smallest and simplest projects to fail.

When an organization makes a decision not to do an SOW, it puts the delivery team at high risk for not completing the project successfully. The risk arises when changes start occurring on the project and there's no baseline document for the team to reference to determine when a change has actually occurred. In addition, the team has little proof to justify charging the client additional fees to cover the out-of-scope work when they can't prove that the work is truly out-of-scope. Even the smallest changes can turn into very big ones if they're not managed properly. If there are a large number of these projects across the organization, they could lead to a major financial setback.

The following case study provides a description of a small, simple project for which a sample SOW will be developed.

Company USA, a small engineering and design firm with approximately 100 employees, has been experiencing ever-increasing problems in bringing projects in on schedule and within budget. The majority of Company USA's projects range from $200,000 to $400,000 and typically take 6 to 12 months to complete. The average gross profit (GP) margin historically realized on its projects has been around 40 percent. However, this margin has continually decreased over the past two years to a new low average GP of 10 percent.

Company USA has been receiving feedback from clients providing overwhelming evidence that the cause for the project failures was very poor project management skills in the organization. Company USA realized that they had to do something to improve the way they managed projects, but they didn't know where to start. After some research, they found that APEX Consulting had recently developed a project management maturity model to help organizations determine where their project management processes were deficient and, in turn, identify key areas to improve upon to reach the next level of maturation.

Company USA was starting to feel the financial pressure that the mismanaged projects were placing on its bottom line, so it was important to correct the situation as quickly as possible. To expedite the process, Company USA decided to forgo a competitive bidding process and instead opted to have APEX Consulting submit a noncompetitive proposal for doing an analysis of its organization. As part of the proposal, APEX Consulting prepared a proposal SOW (PSOW) to define the scope of the analysis to be conducted. APEX Consulting informed Company USA that it generally required some period of time to do due diligence prior to signing a contract with a client. However, if Company USA insisted that the contract be signed based on the proposal, then the PSOW would be considered to be the contract SOW (CSOW) and as such would serve as the baseline for any future changes. In addition, the cost to perform the maturity analysis would be billed on a time and materials (T&M) basis to compensate for any unforeseen risks due to the lack of a proper due diligence analysis. Company USA accepted these conditions and awarded the contract to APEX Consulting with one stipulation: The analysis had to be completed within two months after initiation.

The following is a sample CSOW for the project management maturity analysis to be performed by APEX Consulting for Company USA.

Contract Statement of Work

For

COMPANY USA

PROJECT MANAGEMENT MATURITY ANALYSIS PROJECT

APEX Consulting
Atlanta, GA

TABLE OF CONTENTS

12 ATTACHMENTS
   12.1 CHANGE ORDER REQUEST FORM
   12.2 SAMPLE REPORTS
      12.2.1 Project Status Report
      12.2.2 Project Management Maturity Analysis Report

1 STATEMENT OF CONFIDENTIALITY

APEX Consulting acknowledges that the information contained in this document is confidential and proprietary to Company USA. APEX Consulting agrees to use the same level of care to protect the confidentiality of this information as it uses to protect its own.

This document contains processes, techniques, and methodologies that are proprietary to APEX Consulting and are provided to the customer with the understanding that this information will be used for planning, executing, controlling, and closing the project described in this document.

Each recipient of this document is expected to treat this information with the strictest confidence and is responsible for ensuring that there is no unauthorized duplication, distribution, or application of this material, unless expressly stated in this SOW.

2 INTRODUCTION

2.1 Purpose

The purpose of this Contract Statement of Work (CSOW) is to document the service to be delivered, the price of the requested service, and the rights and responsibilities of the various parties responsible for delivery. This service has been requested by Company USA to meet its objective of improving profitability on its projects by determining its current level of project management maturity and identifying areas for improving the processes and procedures currently being used to manage projects. This document also addresses the specific requirements of Company USA, as well as the specific requirements of APEX Consulting to deliver the requested services properly.

Upon acceptance by both Company USA and APEX Consulting, any changes or modifications to the SOW must follow the change control process defined in Section 5.1 of this SOW. All approved changes will become attachments to the original approved CSOW, which will then form the new baseline upon which future changes will be measured.

2.2 Description of Work

APEX Consulting will perform a project management maturity analysis for Company USA, an engineering and design firm headquartered in Atlanta, GA, to assist Company USA in identifying areas for improving the processes and procedures used for managing projects. This analysis will consist of reviewing Company USA's current project management processes, procedures, tools, and documents. The information gathered from this review will then be used to develop an initial maturity rating of Company USA's project management skills. A detailed description of the maturity analysis is provided in Section 3.0 of this SOW.

2.3 Assumptions

1. APEX Consulting will adhere to the standards of conduct as defined in Company USA's and APEX Consulting's Standard Code of Conduct
2. Company USA will provide APEX Consulting with the required office space for performing the analysis, as defined in Section 7 of this SOW
3. Company USA will provide on-site parking for all APEX Consulting personnel performing analysis work outside the standard hours of operation, as defined in Section 6 of this SOW.

4. Company USA will be responsible for all costs incurred by APEX Consulting for obtaining all necessary security clearances required by Company USA, including the cost of background checks and drug screening.

> **Lessons Learned:** This section is typically reserved for assumptions that cover more than one service being provided to a client. In situations like this where there is only one service being delivered, it is important that only those assumptions that are general in nature and not specific to the service be addressed. One way to make this determination is to ask the questions: Would the assumption apply regardless of the service being offered? Or is it specifically required to deliver a particular service? If the assumption is specific to the service, then it should be covered in Section 3; otherwise, it should be covered here as a general assumption.

2.4 Constraints

1. Security access required at Company USA's office could delay the APEX Consulting personnel in obtaining the necessary information for the analysis.
2. APEX Consulting will not be allowed to perform any due diligence prior to execution of the contract.
3. Company USA has requested that the analysis be conducted as expeditiously as possible, which may limit the detail to which some of the areas may be analyzed.

3 SERVICES PROVIDED

3.1 Project Management Maturity Analysis

3.1.1 Description

APEX Consulting will perform a project management maturity analysis of Company USA to determine the organization's level of maturity in managing projects. This analysis will also identify areas for improving processes and procedures currently being used to manage projects. The analysis will be conducted in four phases:

- Phase 1: Planning
- Phase 2: Data Collection
- Phase 3: Data Analysis
- Phase 4: Reporting.

During the Planning phase, APEX Consulting and Company USA will jointly define the scope and develop a plan for performing the analysis. Once the scope has been defined and the planning is completed, the analysis will then move into the Data Collection phase. During this phase, APEX Consulting will collect data on Company USA's current project management processes, procedures, and tools. The data collection will be conducted through questionnaires and interviews of a select number of employees, as determined during the planning phase. It is anticipated that the number of employees receiving the questionnaires and being interviewed will not exceed 20% of the total base number of employees at the time of project initiation. APEX will also gather data by reviewing Company USA's administrative and project documents.

After all the data have been collected, the analysis will move into the Data Analysis phase, during which APEX Consulting will aggregate the information and analyze it to develop the initial maturity rating for Company USA. The maturity rating will be based on APEX Consulting's proprietary five-level project management maturity model:

- Level 1 – Emerging
- Level 2 – Standardization
- Level 3 – Acceptance
- Level 4 – Cultural
- Level 5 – Optimizing.

Once the data have been analyzed, APEX will develop a report of its findings and submit it to Company USA as the final project deliverable. This report will be titled the *Project Management Maturity Analysis Report*. Development and delivery of the report to Company USA will be conducted in the fourth and final phase of the analysis, Reporting.

At the request of Company USA, the maturity analysis must be completed within two months after initiation of the planning phase.

3.1.2 Key Assumptions

1. Company USA will provide personnel to assist APEX Consulting in defining the scope and developing the plan for performing the analysis.
2. Company USA will provide a current list of all employees, including their functional title, years of experience, phone number, and e-mail address. To ensure the confidentiality of the information gathered, APEX Consulting will not use the names of the employees in the analysis.
3. APEX Consulting will not be held to the scheduled completion date of the analysis when delays are attributed to Company USA or its employees.
4. Company USA will provide all information requested by APEX Consulting to conduct the maturity analysis properly.
5. The number of employees receiving questionnaires and being interviewed will not exceed 20% of the total base number of employees at the time of project initiation.
6. The maturity analysis will be completed within two months after initiation of the planning phase.

3.1.3 Roles and Responsibilities

The roles and responsibilities of both Company USA and APEX Consulting in performing the project management maturity analysis are as follows:

PM Maturity Analysis—Roles and Responsibilities	APEX Consulting	Company USA
1. Define the scope and develop a plan for performing the maturity analysis	✓	✓
2. Provide a list of all employees, including functional title, years of experience, phone number, and e-mail address		✓

continues

continued

3. Provide office space for APEX Consulting's review team, as defined in Section 7 of the SOW		✓
4. Perform the PM maturity analysis	✓	
5. Develop the PM Maturity Analysis Report	✓	

3.1.4 Service Level Agreements (SLAs)

Not Applicable

> **Lessons Learned:** This service offering does not have established service levels for determining the performance of the service provider. When the CSOW is finalized, the sections that are identified as not applicable (N/A) can be deleted. However, these sections should be included in the initial draft to show reviewers that they were not overlooked.

3.1.5 Deliverables

APEX Consulting will deliver a Project Management Maturity Analysis Report to Company USA as the final deliverable for this project. This report will document the findings of APEX Consulting's analysis and will provide an initial rating of Company USA's project management maturity. The report will also provide recommendations for areas of improvement required for Company USA to move up to the next level of maturation.

4 GENERAL ROLES AND RESPONSIBILITIES

4.1 Corporate Responsibilities

4.1.1 Company USA's Responsibilities

- Company USA will provide the necessary access to its office, including security access, employee/visitor badges, and parking passes.
- Company USA will provide all information and access to knowledge holders required for APEX Consulting to fully perform the maturity analysis described in Section 3 of this SOW.

4.1.2 APEX Consulting

- APEX Consulting will perform the project management maturity analysis of Company USA within the mutually agreed upon time frame defined in Section 9 of this SOW.
- APEX Consulting will comply with the standards of conduct defined in both Company USA's and APEX Consulting's Standard Code of Conduct.
- APEX Consulting will be responsible for selecting and managing APEX Consulting personnel required to perform the maturity analysis.

5 MANAGEMENT PROCEDURES

5.1 Change Control Process

A Change Order Request Form must be completed for all changes requested by either APEX Consulting or Company USA that impact or deviate from the approved SOW. The APEX Consulting Project Manager will be responsible for managing all change order requests submitted on the project in accordance with the following process:

1. All change order requests must be submitted in writing to the APEX Consulting Project Manager either by e-mail or hard copy to be recognized as a formal request. Verbal requests or voice mails will not be considered formal change order requests. The Change Order Request Form, shown in Section 12.1 of this SOW, should be used to document in detail the change and provide justification for why it is needed. The initial submission must also document the estimated work effort and cost specifically for investigating what it would take to implement the change if approved. The cost of any investigation APEX Consulting conducts related to any change requests submitted by Company USA will be billed to Company USA on a time and materials basis, unless otherwise noted or agreed to.

2. Based on the estimated work effort and cost, representatives from both Company USA and APEX Consulting will jointly determine whether to proceed with the investigation. The approval levels established for both Company USA and APEX Consulting are as follows:

APEX Consulting—Approval Limits

Title:	Changes Up to:
Project Manager	$10,000
Regional Director of Services	$50,000
Senior VP of Services	Over $50,000

Company USA—Approval Limits

Title:	Changes Up to:
Chief of Engineering	$50,000
President	Over $50,000

If the investigation is rejected, then the change order request is considered rejected, and no further action is required. If it is accepted, then the requester (or its assignees) will then determine the impact of implementing the change on the project.

3. In investigating the impact of the change on the project, the requester (or its assignees) will determine the impact on the cost, schedule, and manpower originally estimated for the project. The requester will also determine the impact on the SOW and any revisions to the language that may be required, as well as the estimated work effort and cost to implement the change. Once the investigation has been completed, the requester will complete the Change Order Request Form with the information gathered in this step and resubmit it to the project manager for coordinating the review and approval.

4. Based on the estimated work effort and cost, representatives from both Company USA and APEX Consulting will jointly determine whether to proceed with implementing the change. The approval levels required for both Company USA and APEX Consulting are shown in step 2 above. If the implementation is rejected, then the change order request is considered rejected, and no further action is required. If the implementation is accepted, the change order request is considered approved. Once all appropriate signatures have been obtained, the approved change order will then be attached, as an amendment, to the SOW. The amended SOW will become the new baseline document upon which any new changes will be based.

5.2 Meetings

Company USA and APEX Consulting will jointly participate in various meetings to review the progress of the project. The following table identifies the type of meeting, frequency, and proposed attendees.

Type of Meeting	Frequency	Company USA Attendees	APEX Consulting Attendees
Project Kick-off	Once at the beginning of the project	President/Chief of Engineering/other invited Company USA employees	Regional Director of Services/ Project Manager/ maturity analysis team members
Weekly Status Meeting	Every Tuesday from 9:00 a.m.– 11:00 am.	Chief of Engineering/other invited Company USA employees	Project Manager/ team members (as necessary)

5.3 Billing Process

The billing process for this engagement is as follows:

- APEX Consulting will invoice Company USA on a time and materials basis as incurred in arrears. Invoices will be submitted to Company USA's Accounts Payable in electronic or paper form on the 2nd Monday of the month.
- Travel and other related expenses will be invoiced as defined in Section 10.3 of this SOW.
- Company USA's accounts payable representative(s) will process the checks for the services rendered and will mail them to APEX Consulting's headquarters office in Atlanta, GA.
- Invoices will be paid on a net thirty (30) day basis. Company USA will pay a one (1) percent per month charge on all past due invoices.

5.4 Dispute Resolution Process

Any disputes that may arise between Company USA and APEX Consulting during delivery of the requested services will be addressed through the following process:

Step 1: All issues or disputes that cannot be resolved by those involved will be escalated to APEX Consulting's project manager and Company USA's Chief of Engineering.

Step 2: If the parties identified in step 1 cannot resolve the issue or dispute, then it will be escalated to APEX Consulting's Regional Director of Services and Company USA's President.

Step 3: If the parties identified in step 2 cannot resolve the issue or dispute, then an independent party will be brought in to mediate and arbitrate the resolution of the issue or dispute.

Step 4: If the independent arbitrator fails to reach a resolution, then the parties may choose to proceed to litigation. This is the least desirable option, and it should be avoided if at all possible.

5.5 Reports

APEX Consulting will be responsible for producing the reports identified below. A sample of each report is provided in Section 12.2 of this SOW. APEX Consulting will produce customized or ad hoc reports only upon written request from Company USA. The time required to design and develop the customized or ad hoc reports will be charged to Company USA on a time and materials basis.

Report Type	Frequency
Project Status Report	Weekly
Project Management Maturity Analysis Report [Final Project Deliverable]	Once at the end of the project

6 HOURS OF OPERATION

The standard hours of operation for the project management maturity analysis of Company USA are from 8:00 a.m. to 5:00 p.m. Eastern Standard Time (EST), Monday through Friday. This also defines the standard business day for APEX Consulting.

APEX Consulting will observe all Company USA holidays listed below. Company USA will be responsible for notifying APEX Consulting, in writing, prior to initiation of the planning phase of the dates on which each of these holidays will be observed.

- New Year's Day
- Martin Luther King Day
- Presidents Day
- Memorial Day
- Independence Day
- Labor Day
- Veterans Day
- Thanksgiving Day and the day after
- Christmas Day.

If Company USA's office is closed for any reason, such as weather, health concerns, safety, or special events, then APEX Consulting will be relieved of its obligation to deliver the final findings report at the scheduled completion date. Company USA will also be responsible for reimbursing APEX Consulting for any costs or expenses incurred due to an unscheduled closing.

7 FACILITIES/TOOLS/EQUIPMENT REQUIREMENTS

The following are the minimum facility requirements APEX Consulting needs to deliver the services identified in this SOW properly. Company USA will be responsible for ensuring that these facilities are provided to APEX Consulting prior to work being initiated and that the facilities will be at least equivalent to those provided to Company USA's own employees. Company USA will also be responsible for all costs associated with acquisition and use of the facilities, including all charges for the installation and use of phones and modem lines. All facilities provided to APEX Consulting must meet the minimum handicap requirements as defined by the Americans with Disabilities Act of 1990 and the Occupational Safety and Health Act of 1970. Failure to meet these minimum facility requirements will inhibit APEX Consulting's ability to perform the project management maturity analysis within the desired time frame.

Facilities provided to APEX Consulting will only be accessible to its employees and authorized Company USA personnel. To ensure the confidentiality of the information collected, the office areas provided will be fitted with locks, card key entry, and/or electronic security pads for security purposes. Company USA will also provide APEX Consulting with access to conference rooms, cafeterias, parking, health club facilities, and other similar facilities at no charge or at a charge commensurate with that charged to Company USA's own employees. No specific tools are required for the work.

APEX Consulting requires the following facilities and equipment to perform the requested maturity analysis properly:

Facility/Tool/Equipment	Description
Management Office Space	One enclosed office, minimum 100 sq. ft., for the Project Manager. Office to include, at a minimum, a desk, chair, trash can, lights (desk and overhead), two visitor chairs, and two 3-drawer filing cabinets.
Analysis Team Office Space	A separate cubicle, minimum of 64 sq. ft., for each member of the analysis team. Cubicle to include, at a minimum, a desk, chair, trash can, desk light, and 3-drawer filing cabinet.
Interview Rooms	Two rooms, minimum 81 sq. ft. each, to conduct employee interviews. Each room to include, at a minimum, a desk or table and 4 chairs.

continues

continued

Analog Data Lines	Minimum of one modem line for each enclosed office and cubicle provided.
Telephone Lines w/ Phones	Minimum of one phone line with phone for each enclosed office and cubicle provided.
Fax Machines	Access to fax machine.
Printers	Access to laser jet printer (or equivalent).
Copy Machines	Access to copy machine.
HVAC	Heating and air conditioning available and working in all work areas being provided.
Lights and Temperature Control	Lights and temperature control available and working in all work areas.

8 SECURITY REQUIREMENTS

8.1 Facilities

Company USA will provide APEX Consulting with a list of all areas within Company USA's office that require security access for its employees to perform the maturity analysis. The list will also address the type of security access required for each area identified.

8.2 Personnel

Company USA will provide security access to APEX Consulting personnel for all areas requiring it within five (5) business days of the assigned start date. If security clearance is not provided within the five (5) business days, Company USA will provide an escort for the APEX employee requiring access to a secure area. Company USA will cover all costs associated with obtaining the security clearances, including background checks, drug screening, and any other checks or tests required.

9 SCHEDULE

The following table identifies the completion date of the major milestones identified in the initial schedule for performing the project management maturity analysis for Company USA. Upon approval of the CSOW and the contract, these dates will become the baseline schedule upon which future changes will be measured.

Major Milestone	Completion Date
Contract and CSOW approved	1 June 20XX
Planning Phase Completed	15 June 20XX
Data Collection Phase Completed	1 July 20XX
Data Analysis Phase Completed	15 July 20XX
Reporting Phase Completed[1]	31 July 20XX

1. This milestone includes the completion and delivery of the Project Management Maturity Analysis Report to Company USA.

10 PRICING

10.1 Service Pricing Assumptions

Pricing for performing the project management maturity analysis for Company USA is based upon the following data and assumptions documented throughout this SOW:

1. The number of employees to receive questionnaires and to be interviewed will not exceed 20% of the total base number of employees in Company USA at the time of project initiation.
2. The Project Management Maturity Report will be the only deliverable provided to Company USA.
3. Maturity analysis must be completed within two (2) months from initiation of the planning phase.
4. APEX Consulting will not perform work outside the scope defined in this document to correct deficiencies found during the analysis. Company USA may, however, increase the scope to include this additional work by formally submitting a change order request.

Pricing for the delivery of the requested services is structured into the following categories: time and material rates, travel and expenses, shipping fees, and termination fees.

10.2 Time and Materials

The maturity analysis will be billed on a time and materials basis using the rates shown in the table below. APEX Consulting will also assist Company USA with special projects on a time and materials basis, contingent upon sufficient resources being available to meet the request.

APEX Consulting Functional Role	Hourly Rate
Junior Consultant	$65.00
Senior Consultant	$90.00
Project Manager	$150.00
Regional Director of Services	$225.00

10.3 Travel and Expenses

APEX Consulting will bill Company USA for all travel-related expenses incurred in the course of performing the analysis. Travel expenses to be reimbursed by Company USA are as follows:

- $0.36 per mile when using personal auto
- $150/day per diem (covers lodging and meals)
- Actual cost incurred for other travel related expenses, plus a 9% service charge. This includes expenses for phone calls, taxis, rental cars, dry cleaning, and airfares.

10.4 Shipping Fees

If APEX Consulting is required to use an overnight or express delivery service to perform the analysis, the cost for such services will be billed to Company USA as incurred. APEX Consulting will use Company USA's preferred delivery vendor for the shipping services.

10.5 Termination Fees

If Company USA terminates the contract without cause or for convenience, the termination fee will be $100,000.

11 SIGNATURE BLOCK

APEX Consulting   **Company USA**

_____   _____

Date:_____   Date:_____

Senior VP of Services   President

_____   _____

Date:_____   Date:_____

Regional Director of Services   Chief of Engineering

12 ATTACHMENTS

12.1 Change Order Request Form

<table>
<tr><td colspan="2">CHANGE ORDER REQUEST FORM</td><td colspan="2">Change Order No.</td></tr>
<tr><td colspan="4" align="center">SECTION 1 - PROJECT INFORMATION</td></tr>
<tr><td align="right">Client Name:</td><td></td><td align="right">Project Name:</td><td></td></tr>
<tr><td align="right">Project Manager:</td><td></td><td align="right">Project Number:</td><td></td></tr>
<tr><td align="right">PM's Phone Number:</td><td></td><td></td><td></td></tr>
<tr><td colspan="4" align="center">SECTION 2 - CHANGE REQUEST INFORMATION</td></tr>
<tr><td align="right">Initiated by:</td><td></td><td align="right">Date Submitted:</td><td></td></tr>
<tr><td align="right">Initiator's Phone Number:</td><td></td><td align="right">Date Completed:</td><td></td></tr>
<tr><td align="right">Description of Change Request:</td><td colspan="3"></td></tr>
<tr><td align="right">Justification for Change Request:</td><td colspan="3"></td></tr>
<tr><td colspan="4" align="center">SECTION 3 - CHANGE REQUEST INVESTIGATION DECISION</td></tr>
<tr><td align="right">Estimated Work Effort to Investigate:</td><td></td><td align="right">Actual Work Effort to Investigate:</td><td></td></tr>
<tr><td align="right">Estimated Cost to Investigate:</td><td></td><td align="right">Actual Cost to Investigate:</td><td></td></tr>
<tr><td>☐ Investigation Accepted</td><td>Client Representative(s):</td><td></td><td>Date:</td></tr>
<tr><td>☐ Investigation Rejected</td><td>Service Provider Representative(s):</td><td></td><td>Date:</td></tr>
<tr><td>Reason for Rejection:</td><td colspan="3"></td></tr>
<tr><td colspan="4" align="center">SECTION 4 - CHANGE REQUEST IMPLEMENTATION DECISION</td></tr>
<tr><td colspan="4" align="center">Impact of Change Request on SOW</td></tr>
<tr><td align="center">SOW Section</td><td colspan="3" align="center">Impact/Change</td></tr>
<tr><td></td><td colspan="3"></td></tr>
<tr><td></td><td colspan="3"></td></tr>
<tr><td></td><td colspan="3"></td></tr>
<tr><td>Category of Change</td><td>From</td><td colspan="2">To</td></tr>
<tr><td>Cost</td><td></td><td colspan="2"></td></tr>
<tr><td>Schedule</td><td></td><td colspan="2"></td></tr>
<tr><td>Manpower</td><td></td><td colspan="2"></td></tr>
<tr><td align="right">Estimated Work Effort to Implement:</td><td></td><td align="right">Actual Work Effort to Implement:</td><td></td></tr>
<tr><td align="right">Estimated Cost to Implement:</td><td></td><td align="right">Actual Cost to Implement:</td><td></td></tr>
<tr><td>☐ Implementation Accepted</td><td>Client Representative(s):</td><td></td><td>Date:</td></tr>
<tr><td>☐ Implementation Rejected</td><td>Service Provider Representative(s):</td><td></td><td>Date:</td></tr>
</table>

12.2 Sample Reports

12.2.1 Project Status Report

[Insert the customized Project Status Report for this project here.]

12.2.2 Project Management Maturity Analysis Report

[Insert the customized Project Management Maturity Analysis Report for this project here. Any additional reports that are required as part of this project should also be included in this section.]

In reviewing the SOWs for both the complex and simple projects, we see that although the level of detail captured in the two documents varies significantly, the overall structure and look of the SOWs are very similar.

As discussed in Chapter 6, having a common framework and approach for developing the SOW is a critical step for an organization in improving the quality of the documents being produced. Not only do the common framework and approach make it easier to draft the content, but they also provide the development teams with a framework that can be applied to any type and size of project. As the common framework and approach become more ingrained in the organization, a significant amount of knowledge will be generated and will be available to future development teams drafting SOWs for similar projects. The application of this knowledge will improve the profitability of the projects being delivered to the clients as well as overall client satisfaction. In addition, the likelihood of internal projects being delivered under budget and ahead of schedule would improve.

Enough can't be said about the importance of having a common framework and approach in place for developing SOWs. Nonetheless, if the framework and approach are not supported by the executive leadership and practiced throughout the organization, they won't be worth the paper they're written on. To realize the benefits of the SOW, the framework and approach have to be institutionalized and become part of the organization's culture for managing projects. When this happens, the organization will be well on its way to becoming world-class at delivering successful projects.

Part 3

Maintaining the SOW for Project Excellence

Chapter 9

Managing Change to the SOW

It's a bad plan that can't be changed.

—*Publilius Syrus*

As noted in Chapter 2, one of the three main reasons for project failure is changing requirements and specifications. Change, in and of itself, will not cause a project to fail. Rather, it is an organization's inability to manage change properly that will ultimately lead to a project's demise. Regardless of how much planning is performed on a project, there is always the potential for changes to occur.

Whenever I get an opportunity to speak on the topic of change management, one of the things I stress to the audience is the importance of managing *all* changes on the project, regardless of whether they're large or small, or whether or not a fee is being charged to implement the changes. To describe the importance of managing all changes, I like to use an analogy, which I refer to as the *Power of the Penny*. The audience is asked to choose between the following two scenarios:

1. Receive $1,000 a day for 31 days
2. Receive a single penny on day 1 and allow the sum total to double each day for the next 31 days.

The mathematically challenged will typically choose option 1, which would provide them with $31,000 at the end of the 31 days. However, those who are little more astute in mathematics realize that if the sum total is allowed to double each day it will grow exponentially over the next 31 days. Thus, they choose option 2, which would provide them with the extraordinary sum of $10,737,418.24 (see Figure 9-1).

The purpose of this exercise is to illustrate that even small changes on a project can grow to become very large if left unmanaged. If a project team does not take the time to manage all changes on a project, large and small, the negative financial impact can become quite substantial over time. This also applies to changes made to the project on a *pro bono* basis.

> *If a project team does not take the time to manage all changes on a project, large and small, the negative financial impact can become quite substantial over time.*

It's not uncommon for a client to request that the service provider make minor adjustments to the scope of the work being performed without charging additional fees. Service providers often agree to do this simply to maintain a good relationship with the client. However, doing so sets a precedent that is difficult to break the next time the client makes a request. In addition, when a service provider does this type of work there's a tendency not to document the change, which also means that there's no audit trail showing all changes that have been made to the project. Over time these free changes can add up to a very large sum of money that is not accounted for in the total project cost. Many

1. .01	12. 20.48	23. 41,943.04
2. .02	13. 40.96	24. 83,886.08
3. .04	14. 81.92	25. 167,772.16
4. .08	15. 163.84	26. 335,544.32
5. .16	16. 327.68	27. 671,088.64
6. .32	17. 655.36	28. 1,342,177.28
7. .64	18. 1,310.72	29. 2,684,354.56
8. 1.28	19. 2,621.44	30. 5,368,709.12
9. 2.56	20. 5,242.88	31. 10,737,418.24
10. 5.12	21. 10,485.76	
11. 10.24	22. 20,971.52	

Figure 9-1. Power of the Penny Calculations

organizations simply don't realize how significant an impact these changes can have on the project.

The relationship between the client and the service provider can turn from good to bad very quickly, particularly if there is turnover of key project sponsors or personnel on either side. If a key sponsor from the client leaves the project, his or her replacement may start questioning the value and need for an outside service provider. From the perspective of the service provider, having an audit trail showing all the work that has been done on a *pro bono* basis can show the new client sponsor the value and customer service they have provided to the organization. The ability to provide evidence of all the work that has been done *pro bono* can help improve or solidify the relationship with the client, particularly when there is a new project sponsor. This type of information can translate to higher client satisfaction ratings, opportunities for future work, and perhaps most important, the ability to use the client as a future reference.

THE IMPORTANCE OF MANAGING CHANGE

One of the main responsibilities of the project manager is to maintain a balance among the scope, cost, and schedule of a project. These are generally referred to as a project's *triple constraints* and are often depicted as an equilateral triangle (see Figure 9-2). The SOW establishes the initial parameters for the triangle by defining the baseline

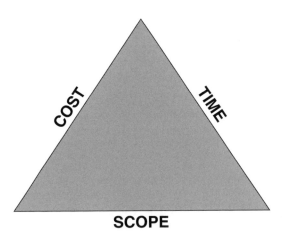

Figure 9-2. Triple Constraint Triangle

scope, cost, and scheduled completion date of the work to be performed for the client. When one side of the triangle is increased or decreased, it will have a direct impact on the other two.

To maintain a balance among these constraints, a detailed change management process must be in place. If changes to any of these constraints are not documented and managed properly, the triangle will get out of balance very quickly. When this happens, the project is heading for trouble. For example, let's consider a scenario where a client has requested that the scope of the project be increased to accommodate some additional work; however, no change order is submitted to increase the time and cost of the project to account for this additional work. Without a change order to increase these factors, the additional scope will essentially be done within the original budget and scheduled completion date established for the project. This means that the cost for performing this additional work will have

> *An organization's failure to manage change on a project can lead to a multitude of problems, including: scope creep, cost and schedule overruns, poor utilization of resources, reduced quality of the product produced, and lost profitability.*

to come from contingency funds or any profit margin anticipated for the project—neither of which would be a good option.

An organization's failure to manage change on a project can lead to a multitude of problems, including: scope creep, cost and schedule overruns, poor utilization of resources, reduced quality of the product produced, and lost profitability. In addition, if either the client or service provider were to seek retribution through the legal system for any negative impacts that a change may have caused without having an approved change order, the likelihood of winning the suit would be very slim.

Several recent court cases have litigated this very issue. In *Miorelli Engineering v. County of Brevard*, Miroelli sued Brevard County, Florida, for breach of contract and sought damages for work they had performed outside the scope of the contract. After going through the trial court and the court of appeals, the case was eventually elevated to the Supreme Court of Florida for a decision. The Supreme Court ruled that Miorelli Engineering could not recover the cost of work it had performed outside the scope of the contract with Brevard County because without a written and approved change order, the county was protected by the sovereign immunity doctrine.[1]

In the case of *Choate Construction v. Ideal Electrical Contractors*, Ideal sued Choate Construction, arguing that the *theory of quantum meruit* allowed them to recover the reasonable value of services performed outside the scope of the contract. The agreement between Choate and Ideal specified that Choate would pay Ideal the amount set forth in the subcontract; however, it also noted that this amount could be increased or decreased for any changes the parties agreed to in writing. The subcontract further specified that Ideal would not be paid for work performed outside the defined scope, unless Choate first authorized it in writing before the work was initiated. Although Ideal won the case in trial court, Choate appealed the decision to the Court of Appeals of Georgia, which reversed the decision. The appellate court ruled that Ideal had accepted the terms of the subcontract; however, Ideal did not follow the change management process for work being performed outside the original scope. Since Ideal did not follow the terms of the contract, it was denied payment for the work under the *theory of quantum meruit*.[2]

Another example of how an organization can be negatively impacted financially by not following an agreed-upon change management process is found in *A.H.A. General Contracting v. New York City Housing Authority*. In this case, A.H.A. General Contracting was awarded two contracts with the New York City Housing Authority—one for $2.3 million and the other for $2.4 million. Each contract specifically required A.H.A. to submit all claims, along with any support documentation, to the Housing Authority in a timely manner. This provision was put in place to allow the Housing Authority time to review the claims to ensure that any additional work performed outside the original scope was justified and that public funds were being spent wisely.

Upon completing the work for both contracts, A.H.A. submitted two claims for additional work that they had performed—$700,513 on the first contract and $205,125 on the second. After reviewing the claims, the Housing Authority recognized only minor adjustments for the additional work and refused to pay the claims in full. A.H.A. sued for breach of contract, seeking payment for the additional work performed. The trial court, as well as the New York Court of Appeals, dismissed A.H.A.'s claims, ruling that it had not met the notice of claims and reporting requirements specified under the two contracts. A.H.A. lost close to $1 million in claims on the two contracts, not including legal fees, simply because it had failed to follow the change management process agreed to in the contract.[3]

These three cases clearly highlight the importance not only of managing change on projects, but also of ensuring that change is managed in accordance with the process defined in the contract or SOW. The impact of failing to do so could easily reach into the billions or trillions of dollars a year on mismanaged projects across all industries.

IDENTIFYING WHEN A CHANGE OCCURS

To manage change to a project properly, one first has to be able to identify when a change is being proposed or has occurred. For the purpose of this discussion, a change is defined as any deviation from the scope agreed to in the CSOW. Any change that is outside the general scope of this document is referred to as a "cardinal change."[4] Three factors must be considered when determining whether a change is significant enough to be classified as a cardinal change:

1. Has, or will, the magnitude of the work to be performed been significantly changed?
2. Is the change requiring the procurement of a totally different product, or is it altering the quality, character, functionality, or type of work defined in the CSOW?
3. Does the cost of the proposed change greatly exceed the baseline cost established in the CSOW?[5]

If the answer to any of these questions is "yes," the proposed change is considered a cardinal change. According to the cardinal change doctrine, clients are generally restricted to requesting changes that are within the general scope defined in the CSOW. If it is determined that a proposed change is a cardinal change, then the service provider will not be required to implement the change unless specific clauses are included in the SOW that address how changes of this nature will be managed.

> *To manage change to a project properly, one first has to be able to identify when a change is being proposed or has occurred.*

This doctrine also has a legal basis. In the case of *Becho, Inc. v. United States*, Becho had contracted with the U.S. Army Corps of Engineers to deliver two separate piles of riprap (stones placed together in an irregular or loose fashion to form a foundation or a wall) to a quarry in Jackson Hole, Wyoming. The contract called for Becho to group the riprap in such a way that breakage would be minimized and the piles would contain materials of dissimilar sizes. The Corps would then pay Becho based on the total number of cubic yards of acceptable material in each pile.[6]

During the course of the project, the Corps determined that some of the material in both piles was unsatisfactory and did not meet the required specifications. The Corps issued a change order that required Becho to remove the unsatisfactory material from the piles and transport it to another location away from the quarry. The change order, however, did not allow for an adjustment in the contract price of the work. Becho agreed to remove the material from the second pile of riprap, but refused to do the work on the first pile since the Corps had already accepted the material and paid for the work.

After removing the material from the second pile, Becho removed its equipment and requested payment for the work. The Corps, however, considered Becho to be in breach of contract because it had not also removed the unsatisfactory material from the first pile. Becho refuted this in court by arguing that the change requested by the Corps was a cardinal change, and Becho was therefore under no obligation to perform the work. The court recognized the cardinal change doctrine, noting that it did not obligate the contractor to perform work that was outside the general scope of the contract. Becho survived the Corps' initial legal challenge; however, at the time of this writing, the issue had not been fully resolved regarding whether the Corps' actions constituted a cardinal change.[7] This issue could have been avoided if the SOW had contained language or a clause specifying how unsatisfactory material was to be handled, including the cost for removal of any material.

Some SOW development teams will choose to identify elements in the SOW that are considered out of scope. This is essentially a wasted effort that adds no real value to the SOW or the project. Instead, it is best to make it clear to all parties involved in the project that if something is not identified in the SOW, then it's out of scope. The project manager plays an extremely important role in ensuring that this is clearly communicated to all parties involved, as well as ensuring that this criterion is adhered to throughout the life of the project. If this is not done, changes on the project can get out of control very quickly.

> *It is best to make it clear to all parties involved in the project that if something is not identified in the SOW, then it's out of scope.*

The Big Dig, a federal highway project in Boston, Massachusetts, is a great example of what can happen if change is not managed properly. In April 2000, the Federal Highway Administration released an audit report on the project, which identified enormous cost overruns as well as an overall lack of management control. The report concluded that the estimated total cost to complete the project was approximately $14 billion—an increase of $11 billion over the original estimate of $2.6 billion.[8] And this is for a single project! Clearly, the additional expenditures caused by unexpected changes on projects across all industry sectors could easily reach into the trillions of dollars.

FACTORS TO CONSIDER IN MANAGING CHANGES TO THE PROJECT

At first glance, the concept of managing change seems simple. So why do so many organizations have such a hard time with it? The reality is that managing change can be one of the most difficult things to do, particularly if your organization is immature in its project management processes and procedures. The difficulty arises not because the process is technically complex, but because of the challenge of getting the project team members to follow the process. Some of the factors that contribute to a team not managing change properly on a project include:

- Lack of a detailed SOW to establish the baseline information upon which future change will be measured
- Lack of a change management section in the SOW that is understood and accepted by all parties involved in project delivery
- Lack of discipline and rigor among the project team members in adhering to and enforcing the change management process
- Poor communications among the project team regarding when a change has occurred

- Lack of understanding by the project team of what was agreed to in the SOW
- Perception that a change is not significant enough to warrant or justify doing a change order
- Decision by the service provider to perform additional work for the client on a *pro bono* basis, simply to build the client relationship.

Each of these factors can impede the management of changes to a project. Thus, it is important to understand what they involve and how they can be avoided on your projects.

Lack of a Detailed SOW: To say that a detailed SOW is an important factor in managing change on a project is a tremendous understatement. If an SOW doesn't exist on a project, then it is impossible to determine when a change has occurred and therefore to manage that change. It's critical not only to understand when a change occurs, but also to determine how it is impacting the project's scope, schedule, cost, quality, and manpower. If an SOW is not in place that establishes limits on the scope of work to be performed, then essentially all changes made to the project will be in scope.

> *It's critical not only to understand when a change occurs, but also to determine how it is impacting the project's scope, schedule, cost, quality, and manpower.*

In this scenario, the scope of the project could continue to grow out of control. Without an SOW to establish the baseline upon which to measure change, there is no way to manage and quantify the true impact of the changes to the project. Having a detailed SOW in place will help establish a baseline to determine when a change has occurred and to measure its impact on the project.

Lack of a Change Management Section in the SOW: Even if an SOW exists on a project, there is no guarantee that changes will be managed properly. In fact, the SOW can describe the scope of work to be performed in great detail, but if it doesn't address how to determine when a change has occurred—as well as the review and approval process for proposed changes—then it could easily contribute to the mismanagement of changes to the project. For example, language in the complex SOW example in Chapter 8 stated that if the call volume exceeded +/–10% of the call volume identified, then a change order request would be required. This type of quantitative threshold can assist the delivery team in clearly identifying when a change is required, which in turn will help ensure that all changes are properly captured and managed on the project. Having the appropriate change management processes and thresholds in place will help avoid reduced profit margins and unsatisfactory client satisfaction ratings.

Lack of Discipline and Rigor in Enforcing the Change Management Process: Some organizations may have in place a detailed SOW that includes a change management process; however, the team assigned to the project simply isn't following the process defined in the document. This situation is often attributed to the lack of discipline and rigor of the organization, the project manager, or the project team responsible for enforcing the process. If a change process is defined in the SOW, then it is imperative that it be followed. Otherwise, the team will ignore changes that may drastically increase or decrease the scope of the project. Ignoring the changes also means that no adjustments are being made to the cost, scheduled completion date, or manpower.

If you define a change management process and don't follow it, you set a precedent with the team that managing change is not important. The team will ignore the process, leading to scope creep, cost overruns, schedule slips, poor quality, and poor utilization of resources. The change process must be enforced with discipline and rigor if the project is to be successful. The individual leading the project must not only have strong project management skills, but also be well respected by the project team. It is also important that the support for applying the change management process be driven from the executive leadership of the organization down to the individual team members. Visible support from the top will greatly expedite acceptance of the process at lower levels in the organization.

Poor Communications among Project Team Members: Difficulty in managing change on a project can be amplified if there is poor communication among the project team members. If mechanisms are not in place for ensuring that changes are identified and communicated to the appropriate individuals, then the project manager's ability to properly manage changes on the project will be inhibited. To avoid miscommunications, the SOW should address the escalation process for team members identifying or requesting changes. This process will define who can request a change and how to submit the request to the appropriate individuals.

Lack of Understanding about What Was Agreed to in the SOW: The project team often lacks understanding about what was agreed to in the SOW between the client and the service provider. In many cases the SOW has been more or less developed in a vacuum, often between a sales account manager or executive and a client representative. The individuals involved often did a poor job of communicating to the team what was agreed to in the SOW. Some organizations may consider certain information (e.g., labor rates, pricing) to be confidential and not allow even their own personnel access. Thus, they either neglect or refuse to provide the project team with a full copy of the SOW. When this occurs, the team goes into the project blind, not knowing what has been agreed to or even what deliverables or service levels are to be achieved during delivery of the project.

A simple way to avoid this type of miscommunication is to provide each of the team members a cleansed copy of the approved SOW with information specific to their area of responsibility. The cleansed version of the SOW would simply delete those sections considered to be confidential or proprietary and outside the group's area of responsibility or need to know. Once the team members are aware of what is to be delivered as part of the project, they will be able to determine when a change has occurred or when a proposed change may impact the agreed-upon SOW. This awareness will help ensure that all changes to the project are captured and properly documented.

Perception That a Change Is Not Significant Enough to Justify a Change Order: Sometimes a change will be proposed that may seem so small or insignificant that it doesn't justify going through the complete change management process. Teams often state that it will cost more to go through the process than it will to implement the change. Although this may be true on a particular case, the justification does not stand up when considering the impact of the aggregate of all similar changes. As noted in the penny analogy, small changes can ultimately grow to represent a substantial sum if they're left unmanaged. A change may seem small or insignificant at the time it is proposed,

> *A change may seem small or insignificant at the time it is proposed, but it can have a cascading impact on other parts of the project that may not be fully realized until later in the project.*

but it can have a cascading impact on other parts of the project that may not be fully realized until later in the project. The resulting delay could lead to rework, schedule and cost overruns, and a reduced profit margin for the service provider. The cumulative effect of these changes could even lead to project failure. Thus, it is imperative that all changes be documented and managed according to the agreed-upon change management process, regardless of their size.

Performing Additional Work for the Client on a Pro Bono Basis: As noted, clients will often ask that small changes be made to the project on a pro bono basis. If the work is being done for free, teams will tend to neglect processing a change order. Lack of a change order causes the project to have a false baseline upon which to measure future changes. If the changes aren't documented and managed properly, they could ultimately harm the project.

TOOLS FOR MANAGING CHANGE TO THE PROJECT

To manage change properly, standard processes and tools must be in place for documenting and tracking changes to the project. For the purpose of this discussion, we will define a tool as a customized template or form used by the project manager in managing change. In addition to the SOW, two primary tools should be used for managing changes on projects: (1) Change Order Request Form, and (2) SOW Change Order Tracker.

Change Order Request Form

The Change Order Request Form is typically customized to meet an organization's specific change management requirements. Despite the lack of a recognized standard, certain fields of information should be captured for every change order requested on a project. These include: the change order number; a description of the change; the justification for the change; the estimated cost to investigate the feasibility and value of implementing the change; the impact of the change on the SOW; the impact on the cost, schedule, and manpower of the project; the estimated cost of implementing the change; and an approval section for both the investigation and implementation. This information is applicable in managing change regardless of the industry, organization, or type of project being performed.

The sample Change Order Request Form provided in Figure 9-3 illustrates one possible format that may be used for capturing the required information. This form is divided into four sections:

- Section 1—Project Information
- Section 2—Change Request Information
- Section 3—Change Request Investigation Decision
- Section 4—Change Request Implementation Decision.

Section 1—Project Information: This section of the form is where the basic project information is captured. It includes the client's name, the project manager's name and phone number, the project name, and the project number (if applicable). The section also includes the change order request number, which is critical for tracking and auditing the number and types of changes made to a project. Organizations that are at a low level of maturity in their project management processes may simply number the change orders in ascending numerical order. However, if a project manager is managing multiple projects, it can be very easy to confuse the change order requests from the various projects. To avoid any potential confusion, the organization or project manager may develop a specific code unique to each project.

For example, let's assume that a change order request is being submitted for the complex SOW supporting the Galaxy Telecommunications IT outsourcing project described in Chapter 8. Let's also assume that service provider (APEX Consulting) is very mature in project management and in managing changes to the project. Therefore, they may have a change order coding structure as follows: full or partial name of the client-CO (change order)-change order number. Following this structure, the first change order for the project would be Galaxy-CO-0001. When managing multiple projects, having an established coding structure in place that is unique and specific to each project will help avoid the confusion that may occur where only an ascending list of numbers is used.

CHANGE ORDER REQUEST FORM		Change Order No.

SECTION 1 - PROJECT INFORMATION			
Client Name:		Project Name:	
Project Manager:		Project Number:	
PM's Phone Number:			

SECTION 2 - CHANGE REQUEST INFORMATION			
Initiated by:		Date Submitted:	
Initiator's Phone Number:		Date Completed:	
Description of Change Request:			
Justification for Change Request:			

SECTION 3 - CHANGE REQUEST INVESTIGATION DECISION				
Estimated Work Effort to Investigate:		Actual Work Effort to Investigate:		
Estimated Cost to Investigate:		Actual Cost to Investigate:		
☐ Investigation Accepted	Client Representative(s):		Date:	
☐ Investigation Rejected	Service Provider Representative(s):		Date:	
Reason for Rejection:				

SECTION 4 - CHANGE REQUEST IMPLEMENTATION DECISION				
Impact of Change Request on SOW				
SOW Section	Impact/Change			
Category of Change	From		To	
Cost				
Schedule				
Manpower				
Estimated Work Effort to Implement:		Actual Work Effort to Implement:		
Estimated Cost to Implement:		Actual Cost to Implement:		
☐ Implementation Accepted	Client Representative(s):		Date:	
☐ Implementation Rejected	Service Provider Representative(s):		Date:	

Figure 9-3. Change Order Request Form

Section 2—Change Request Information: The information captured in this section identifies who initiated the request and when it was submitted, and also provides a description and justification of the change. Knowing when the change order request was submitted is an important element in tracking the status of the request as it progresses through the various levels of approval. The description should be a detailed narrative of no more than a paragraph or two that clearly defines the change being proposed to the project. The justification section should explain why this change is needed and important to the success of the project. It should also describe the value and benefits that will be gained if the change is approved and implemented.

Section 3—Change Request Investigation Decision: This section addresses the estimated work effort and cost associated with investigating what it will take to implement a proposed change. Organizations, particularly service providers, often do not take into consideration the effort and cost that go into determining whether a proposed change is feasible, and whether it will add value to the project. If the work effort and cost are not quantified for this effort, the service provider could end up absorbing the costs for the investigation. This effort could take anywhere from a couple of days to a couple of weeks and easily run into the tens of thousands of dollars.

The purpose of this section is to ensure that both the client and the service provider are aware of the estimated work effort and cost to be expended on investigating the feasibility, benefits, and cost of implementing the proposed change. Before proceeding with the investigation, both the client and the service provider must sign off on the decision. If both parties agree to the cost, then the group assigned to perform this work will proceed with the investigation. As part of this analysis, the team will develop estimates for the work effort and cost to implement the proposed change. If both parties disapprove of proceeding with the investigation, then the change order request is terminated, and no further work will be required. If the investigation is disapproved, a reason for why it was rejected should be provided at the end of the section. The team can then use this information in the future when considering whether a similar type of change should be made.

This section also allows the project manager to capture the actual work effort and cost associated with investigating the change request. This information is useful primarily for reference in developing future estimates. However, if the actual cost to investigate a change is significantly higher than the estimated value, then the service provider may have to go back to the client for additional funding.

Section 4—Change Request Implementation Decision: The last section of the form captures the information gathered from the investigation approved in Section 3. This includes identifying which section of the SOW is being impacted and how the language in that section should be modified to support the change. In addition, the requester or initiator must provide information on how the change will increase (or decrease) the cost, scheduled completion date, and manpower associated with the project. Based on this analysis, an estimate of the work effort and cost must also be provided. The appropriate representatives from both the client and the service provider will then review the information and make a determination to accept or reject the change order request. If the decision is to reject the change order request, then the request is terminated and no further work will be required. If the decision is to accept the request, then the project team will be given the go-ahead to proceed with the approved changes.

As in Section 3, the form allows the project manager to capture the actual work effort and cost associated with implementation of the change request. This information is captured primarily for reference in developing future estimates for implementing similar changes. If the cost to implement an approved change is significantly higher than the estimated value, then the service provider may have to go back to the client for additional funding to cover the actual expenditures.

To ensure that the project team is fully aware of the requirements and the process for completing a Change Order Request Form, the project manager may consider providing a set of work instructions. These instructions may also be included in the change management section of the SOW. Including them in the SOW also ensures that both the client and the service provider had input into their development and that both agree to the process.

The following is a set of work instructions for completing the sample Change Order Request Form:

CHANGE ORDER REQUEST FORM—WORK INSTRUCTIONS

INSTRUCTION NAME:	Change Order Request Form Work Instructions
SCOPE STATEMENT:	To provide instructions to the project team on how to complete a Change Order Request Form.
WORK INSTRUCTION OWNER:	The project sponsor or the project manager for the project will determine the owner of the

work instructions. This may be an individual or a group who has responsibility for all business processes on a project.

REFERENCES: This section identifies where a copy of the Change Order Request Form can be found in the organization. For example, if the service provider's methodology is on an intranet site, the URL of the site would be provided.

TOOL REQUIREMENTS: Microsoft Word®
Microsoft Visio®

PROCESS STEPS:
1. The Change Order Request Form must be completed by the individual requesting the change and submitted in writing to the project manager. This form should be submitted any time there is a change in the baseline scope, scheduled completion date, cost, or manpower assigned to a project as set forth in the approved SOW.
2. The Change Order Request Form is a Microsoft Word® template, which may be found in one of the references noted above. Once the template has been located, simply open the file and complete each of the following data fields contained in the form:

Section 1—Project Information

• *Change Order Request #*—The coding for the change order request number will be established by the service provider or jointly with the client. The coding structure may be: full or partial name of the client-CO-change order number. Following this structure, the first change order for the complex project discussed in Chapter 8 would be Galaxy-CO-0001. The only thing that would change for subsequent change orders would be the change order number, which would increase in ascending order. The project manager is responsible for tracking and assigning this number to each change order request.

- *Client Name*
- *Project Manager Name and Phone Number*
- *Project Name*
- *Project Number* (if applicable).

Section 2—Change Request Information

- *Name of Initiator and Phone Number.*
- *Description of Change Request*—Provide a brief narrative description of the proposed changes to the project.
- *Justification for Change Request*—Provide a brief justification of why the changes are required, as well as the value and benefits to be gained if the change is approved and implemented.
- *Date Submitted*
- *Date Completed*—Indicate the date the change order received final approval. This date would not be filled in until both the client and the service provider approve the implementation of the change in Section 4.

Section 3—Change Request Investigation Decision

- *Estimated Work Effort to Investigate*—Estimate the number of man-hours, days, etc., required to investigate what it will take to implement the requested change. The decision to accept or reject the investigation will be based on this estimate.
- *Estimated Cost to Investigate*—Estimate the cost to investigate what it will take to implement the requested change. The decision to accept or reject the investigation will be based on this estimate.
- *Actual Work Effort to Investigate*—Indicate the actual number of man-hours, days, etc.,

used to investigate what it would take to implement the requested change. This section is to be completed once the investigation is completed. This information is gathered to help in estimating the cost for similar types of requests in the future.

- *Actual Cost to Investigate*—Indicate the actual cost incurred in investigating what it will take to implement the requested change. This section is to be completed once the investigation is completed. This information is gathered to help in estimating the cost for similar types of requests in the future.

- *Approvals*—Representatives from both the client and the service provider must agree on either accepting or rejecting whether to proceed with investigation of the change order request. Levels of approval authority must be established for both parties. The level of approval required will be based on the estimated cost of the investigation.

- *Investigation Accepted*—Check this box if both parties, at the appropriate level of approval, agree to proceed with the investigation.

- *Investigation Rejected*—Check this box if both parties, at the appropriate level of approval, disagree or reject proceeding with the investigation.

- *Reason for Rejection*—If the decision is made not to proceed with the investigation, provide the reason why the request was rejected.

Section 4—Change Request Implementation Decision

- *Impact of Change Request on SOW:* Indicate the sections of the SOW impacted by the proposed change and the revised language required to support it.

- *Category of Change*—Indicate the current baseline cost, schedule, or manpower data in the "From" column and the revised cost, schedule, or manpower data as a result of the change in the "To" column.
- *Estimated Work Effort to Implement*—Estimate the number of man-hours, days, etc., required to implement the requested change. The decision to accept or reject implementation of the change will be based on this estimate.
- *Estimated Cost to Implement*—Estimate the cost to implement the requested change. The decision to accept or reject implementation of the change will be based on this estimate.
- *Actual Work Effort to Implement*—Indicate the actual number of man-hours, days, etc., used in implementing the requested change. This section is to be completed once implementation is completed. The information will help in estimating the work effort for similar types of requests in the future.
- *Actual Cost to Implement*—Indicate the actual cost incurred in implementing the requested change. This section is to be completed once the implementation is completed. This information is gathered to help in estimating the cost for similar types of requests in the future.
- *Approvals*—Representatives from both the client and the service provider must agree on either accepting or rejecting whether to proceed with implementation of the change order request. Levels of approval authority must be established for both parties. The level of approval required will be based on the estimated cost of implementation.
3. The completed Change Order Request Form, along with the revised schedule (if applicable) and an updated costing/pricing

model (if applicable), should be forwarded to the appropriate levels of both the client and the service provider for approval.

4. Upon final approval, the Change Order Request Form will become an amendment to the SOW and the contract. The revised scope, cost, scheduled completion date, and manpower data elements will then become the current approved baseline for all future changes to the project.

PROCESS USER OR EXECUTIONER: Project Manager

OUTPUTS: Approved and Implemented Change Order

> *How does a project get to be a year behind schedule? One day at a time!*
> —*Anonymous*

SOW Change Order Tracker

The second tool that plays an important role in managing project change is the SOW Change Order Tracker. The purpose of this tool is to assist in tracking all approved changes to the project by capturing them in one comprehensive document. This would include any approved pro bono changes. Having this information in one place provides a powerful perspective to anyone reviewing the evolution of a project's scope, cost, schedule, and manpower from the original baseline estimates to its completion.

Someone once asked, "How does a project get to be a year behind schedule?" The reply was, "One day at a time." Although the answer to this question is simple, it speaks volumes on the importance of tracking change on projects. From the perspective of the project manager, it's easy to focus only on the day's most urgent issue. However, just like in the *Power of the Penny* analogy, day-to-day changes can quickly add up to big changes if left unmanaged.

The Change Order Tracker provides several benefits to both the client and the service provider. First, by having all the information in one location, it allows the project manager or any other individual or group to quickly audit the project to ensure that the final cost is equal to the baseline estimate plus all cost increases attributed to approved change orders. This will ensure that all additional costs were approved by both the client and the service provider and that no costs were arbitrarily added to the project without prior approval. If any disputes arise between the client and the service provider on increases of costs or schedule slips on the project, the Change Order Tracker can be referenced to identify specifically where the change occurred and its impact on the project.

Another benefit of the tool is that service providers, as well as internal delivery teams, can build a detailed knowledge base simply by analyzing and comparing the types of changes on similar projects. The respective groups can then use this information in developing future estimates or proposals for similar types of work. The application of this information on future projects will ensure that the teams are addressing these issues during the planning phase, which should lead to fewer change orders later, during the delivery of the project.

The SOW Change Order Tracker can take many different forms, depending on the needs or preferences of the organization responsible for managing changes to the project. As is the case with the Change Order Request Form, there is no one form that is universally accepted as a global best practice or standard for tracking change. A sample SOW Tracker Form is provided as Figure 9-4. This form captures basically the same information as the change order form. The difference is that it shows the cumulative impact of all approved change orders on the cost, schedule, and manpower in one document.

Regardless of the particular structure or format of the form, a minimum set of information should be captured. Essentially, these are the data elements that correspond to the triple constraints of scope, time, and cost:

- Name of the project
- Baseline cost from the approved SOW
- Baseline scheduled completion date from the approved SOW
- Baseline manpower (number of resources) from the approved SOW
- Change order (CO) number
- Section of the SOW being impacted by the change
- Impact of the change on the language contained in the approved SOW
- Impact of the change on the cost, scheduled completion, and manpower associated with the project.

Project Name:
Baseline Cost ($):
Baseline Scheduled Completion Date:
Baseline Manpower (# of Resources):

CO#	Section in SOW	Change Language in the Section of the SOW		Impact (if applicable)					
		From	To	Cost		Schedule Completion		Manpower	
				From	To	From	To	From	To
1									
2									
3									
4									
5									
6									
7									
8									
9									
10									
11									
12									
13									
14									
15									
16									
17									
18									
19									
20									
21									
22									
23									
24									
25									
26									
27									
28									
29									
30									

Figure 9-4. SOW Change Order Tracker

This information is obtained directly from either the SOW or an approved change order for the project. Thus, the project team doesn't need to generate any additional information.

The process of managing and tracking changes on a project requires a great deal of discipline and rigor on the part of everyone associated with the project. For organizations that are immature in their project management processes and methodologies, implementing a change management process can be a difficult transition. Acceptance of the process and tools can be achieved much more easily if the tools can be seamlessly integrated in a way that they easily transfer the data into each other without requiring additional effort by the team.

Having the processes and tools in place for managing changes to a project is a step in the right direction; however, if no one is using them and applying them correctly to the project, then the effort it takes to get to this point will be wasted. When introducing or implementing a detailed change process, it is important to take into consideration not only the individual transition and acceptance of the process, but also the organizational change that also needs to occur for the process to be accepted and implemented successfully throughout the organization. Achieving acceptance at both the organizational and individual levels is a major factor in ensuring the successful management of change on projects. When this is achieved, tremendous benefits will be realized.

NOTES

[1] "Lack of Change Order Sinks Damage Claim," *Civil Engineering,* August 1998, Volume 68, Number 8, p. 32.

[2] "Subcontractor Cannot Recover Payment For Work Performed Outside of Contract," *Civil Engineering*, July 2001, p. 78.

[3] "Recovery for Unclaimed Work Denied," *Civil Engineering,* March 1999, p. 75.

[4] Michael C. Loulakis and Simon J. Santiago. "Cardinal Change Doctrine Excuses Performance." *Civil Engineering*, September 2001, p. 96.

[5] Ibid.

[6] Ibid.

[7] Ibid.

[8] The Associated Press, "Boston Must Dig Deeper to Pay for 'Big Dig,'" *USA Today*, April 6, 2000, p. 11A.

Part 4

Changing the Paradigm

Chapter 10

Selling the Importance and Benefits of the SOW

The real secret of success is enthusiasm. Yes, more than enthusiasm, I would say excitement. I like to see men get excited. When they get excited, they make a success of their lives.

—Walter Chrysler

The development of an SOW is definitely not one of the most *exciting* topics you'll ever read about. However, if your organization has continually experienced failed projects as a result of improperly defined scope and requirements, or if you've been tasked with developing an SOW for the first time, then it can be an extremely *interesting* topic. If a document can make the management and delivery of a project easier and more successful, the project team will exude an excitement that will be contagious throughout the organization. When one group achieves success, others will immediately become interested in what they're doing and try to replicate it.

In the case of organizations or individuals who have never heard of an SOW, it may be necessary to sell them on the importance of the document in the management of their projects. This chapter discusses how to communicate

If you're developing and applying detailed SOWs to your projects and those projects are coming in on time and within budget, then other members of the organization will become very interested in what you're doing and how you're doing it.

the importance of the SOW to your own organization as well as to your client. It also contains a brief discussion on how to sell the SOW as a service offering and how to use the document to sell additional services.

SELLING THE IMPORTANCE OF THE SOW WITHIN YOUR ORGANIZATION

In organizations where no one has ever heard of or used an SOW before, it may be necessary to sell the executive leadership on the importance of and need for using the document on projects. Too often an organization recognizes the need for an SOW only after it has experienced a significant financial loss on several small projects or one large, highly visible project. These failures become the catalyst that finally drives the organization and its leadership to become passionate about the importance and need for the SOW.

Organizations resist using SOWs on their projects simply because they have never used them before and have been somewhat successful nonetheless. In other words, they've been making money in spite of themselves and the way they've managed projects. However, there's an old saying that "If you play with fire, you will eventually get burned." For those organizations that are selling and delivering projects without an SOW, it's just a matter of time before it comes back to burn them; when it does, it may come in the form of a multimillion dollar loss on a project. Almost without exception, if one project fails, it won't be long before another fails.

Rather than wait for the inevitable catastrophic failure to occur, you should act immediately to mitigate against this event by selling the importance of the SOW to your organization. One way to do this is by telling your executive leadership about the benefits that can be gained by implementing the strategies outlined in this book. Another approach is to take the following steps to build a business case that you can present to the executive leadership to convince them to require that SOWs be developed on all projects.

Step—Perform Due Diligence: The first step is to perform due diligence on how the organization is currently managing projects, with particular emphasis on how it is defining the scope and requirements of the work to be performed. Document if SOWs are currently being used on projects and if so, how they're being used. If SOWs are being used, document whether a standard format is used consistently throughout the organization or whether each SOW is different and unique in its structure and content. If SOWs are not being used, gather documentation on whether each project was successful and, if not, would an SOW have helped reverse this outcome?

During this due diligence phase, gather as much quantitative information as possible to support your case. This information can be in the form of lost revenue or profit, cost and schedule overruns, and numerous change orders. The information and statistics discussed in Chapters 2 and 9 contain evidence on the impact an SOW can have on a project. An SOW can also be a strong motivator for executive leadership to change the way projects are managed.

As part of the due diligence process, it is important to identify those individuals and projects that would benefit from having a detailed SOW, as well as those individuals who may oppose or resist its introduction. Knowing those in opposition will allow you to hit on key points in the business case that address their concerns and apprehensions. Easing the fears and concerns of those in opposition may sway them to support the proposed change. Their support could ultimately determine whether or not the change is approved.

In seeking approval, it is critical that you not only identify the individuals who can approve the required use of the SOW and enforce it in the organization, but also that you understand the process required to receive the approval. If an organization has an established process for approving changes in the way projects are managed, it's important that it be followed. Knowing the rules of the game can help expedite the process and ensure that all organizational requirements have been met in gaining the appropriate approvals.

Step 2—Develop a Business Case: After due diligence has been completed, develop a business case that describes the value and benefits that a standard SOW will bring to the organization. If at all possible, quantify the return on investment that project teams may realize by implementing this process. While this may be difficult to do, any type of quantitative data that supports the use of the SOW will be beneficial in selling the concept to the leadership. Although it may take considerably more effort and time on the front end of the project, significant benefits will be realized later, during delivery of the product or service. These benefits include:

- Reduced change orders
- Reduced rework
- More accurate costs and resource estimates
- More accurate schedules
- Improved client satisfaction
- Improved morale of the project team
- Increased profitability
- Projects completed on time, within budget, and of the quality sought by the client.

Step 3—Present the Business Case for Approval: Once the business case has been completed, a meeting should be held with the executive leadership, identified during the due diligence step, who has approval authority within the organization to require the use of SOWs on all projects. A copy of the business case should be provided to each participant well in advance of the meeting. This will allow everyone sufficient time to review the document and prepare any questions. A decision should be made at the conclusion of the meeting or shortly thereafter about whether SOWs should be required.

Step 4—Enable Change: The organizations or individuals who are championing this effort often will consider the internal selling process to be complete once executive approval has been obtained. However, having executive sign-off alone will not make the change successful. Executive sign-off is really just the go-ahead to implement the concept in the organization. It does not ensure that the individuals responsible for developing the SOW on their projects will understand why they're doing it or even how to draft one correctly.

To complete the internal selling process, individual acceptance of the SOW must be achieved. Gaining acceptance from the individuals who will actually be required to use the document can often be much more challenging than getting the organization's buy-in—even when top management is mandating its use. Each per-

> *Gaining acceptance from the individuals who will actually be required to use the document can often be much more challenging than getting the organization's buy-in—even when top management is mandating its use.*

son must clearly understand how this document and process will make their lives easier and their projects more successful.

The benefits of the SOW can be communicated through many different approaches, including the business case, white papers, and brown bag lunches. Training is also important. Without adequate training, you will end up with a very detailed document and process that no one knows how to use properly. Training the individual team members on how to draft and apply the SOW to projects properly is a critical step toward gaining acceptance. The better someone understands the SOW development process and the language that should or should not be included in the SOW, the more likely they'll be to use it—and to use it properly. In introducing the SOW concept into your organization, it's extremely important to take into consideration the training that will need to be developed to support this effort.

Following these four steps will make the selling process easier. A properly conducted selling effort will make the executive leadership aware of the potential risk that their organization and projects could be facing if they do not have an SOW in place. Once they are aware of this risk, they will be able to make the appropriate changes, thus increasing the likelihood of success for their projects.

SELLING THE IMPORTANCE OF THE SOW TO YOUR CLIENTS

In some cases, a service organization may be very mature in its project management processes and procedures, including its use of SOWs on all projects. However, the client may not be as mature and may question the need for developing a detailed SOW. As noted in Chapter 4, the client is the most important member of the SOW development team. Without client participation and input, the service provider will be drafting a document that may or may not be capturing the client's true needs and requirements. If that is the case, the client will likely be dissatisfied and the project will not be successful.

Initially, clients often resist participating in the development of the SOW for many reasons, including:

- Lack of knowledge and understanding of what the SOW is and how it should be developed and applied on a project
- Lack of available resources to participate in the effort
- Lack of experience on the type of project being delivered.

> *Without client participation and input, the service provider will be drafting a document that may or may not be capturing the client's true needs and requirements. If that is the case, the client will likely be dissatisfied and the project will not be successful.*

Moreover, the client may not really know what it wants out of the project. For example, a client may realize that it is very poor at doing project management. They issue an RFP for assistance in helping raise the level of project management maturity throughout the organization. Although they know they have a problem, they have no idea what needs to be done to correct it and improve the situation. They may resist participating in the SOW development process simply because they have no idea what their needs and requirements are for solving the problem.

When this happens, the service provider may not have a clear understanding of what the client's problem is and what needs to happen to fix it. If the SOW is developed in a vacuum, there's a good chance that it won't address the client's true problem and requirements. When the team starts delivering the project, this will become even more apparent. The scope and requirements in essence become a moving target that the project manager is constantly trying to hit. The resulting change order process may be lengthy and complicated. This could ultimately lead to the project being terminated and deemed unsuccessful.

In situations where the client is not familiar with the need for or purpose of an SOW, it may require some effort to sell the importance of the document. It is critical that the client understand that the document is in its best interests as well as those of the service provider. One of the benefits both parties share is the ability to avoid potential disputes regarding what is to be performed or delivered as part of the project. If the SOW can clearly communicate to the service provider what it is supposed to provide to the client and the client

> *If the SOW can clearly communicate to the service provider what it is supposed to provide to the client and the client clearly understands what is to be provided, this will be a huge step forward in delivering a successful project.*

clearly understands what is to be provided, this will be a huge step forward in delivering a successful project.

In selling the client on the importance of the SOW, focus on the benefits for the client, such as:

- Provides an opportunity to participate and provide input
- Captures requirements in detail
- Provides a baseline document for measuring the performance of the service provider
- Clearly outlines what they will be receiving from this project and how much it will cost
- Clearly defines their obligations to the service provider, including resources, facilities, and funding
- Allows them to budget more accurately for the project.

Each of these benefits will reduce rework and potential disputes later on in the project and increase significantly the likelihood that the project will be completed successfully.

SELLING THE SOW DEVELOPMENT PROCESS AS A SERVICE OFFERING

From the perspective of the service provider, particularly those in management consulting practices, the ability to develop and properly apply an SOW to a project can be a very marketable service. In Rick Page's book, *Hope Is Not a Strategy*, he notes that "successful organizations make habits of things others don't like to do, or don't find time to do."[1] Drafting quality SOWs falls into this category. Lack of an established process and framework, or inexperience in drafting and applying an SOW to a project, can be very frustrating and time-consuming. When organizations or individuals shy away from developing the most important document on a project simply because it may take some time, effort, and planning, they put the project and possibly the

When organizations or individuals shy away from developing the most important document on a project simply because it may take some time, effort, and planning, they put the project and possibly the organization at risk.

organization at risk. A service provider with expertise in this area can bring significant value to a client by relieving it of having to undertake this effort.

SELLING ADDITIONAL SERVICES USING THE SOW

Service organizations typically have some form of business development or sales group responsible for bringing new business into the firm. Often these groups tend to focus on a specific solution or service offering for a client. However, additional services a firm may offer could be beneficial and add value to solving the client's problems. If the sales or marketing group doesn't make the client aware of these services, more than likely the client will not request them.

One way of raising this awareness is through the use of a standard SOW that identifies a firm's entire portfolio of services available to its clients. In Chapter 6, we discussed the importance of having a baseline SOW and the various components (or sections) that can make up its structure. One section in particular dealt with the services and products to be provided to the client. It is in this section that the firm's portfolio of services would be identified.

The importance of this section arises during the initial development of the SOW and its coordination with the client. In the PSOW presented to the client, the service provider may list all services it is capable of delivering, for any project. By listing this portfolio of services, the service provider is essentially giving the client an *à la carte* menu of services from which it can choose. For example, if a client has issued an RFP for a particular service, the initial draft of the SOW would only address the scope of that service. In turn, the remaining portfolio of services listed in the SOW would be labeled not applicable (N/A). However, having all services listed in the initial draft may prompt the client to consider the need for additional services that may be required to address the problem at hand or another one that may be outside the scope of this initiative. In either case, it provides the service provider with the potential for additional revenue.

In addition, the client may be able to procure additional services under one SOW and contract, rather than going through a totally separate procurement process. This can save both money and time, both of which would be better spent directly on a project that will yield a positive return on investment. (Keep in mind that listing all services is typically only done in the initial draft of the SOW. For the final draft or CSOW, all services identified as N/A are deleted.)

Following the step-by-step guidelines and approaches discussed in this chapter will help make selling the importance of the SOW to your internal organization, your clients, and any other stakeholders much easier. As noted, having executive approval doesn't necessarily equate to firmwide acceptance and use of the document. To gain true buy-in, the individual team members and other stakeholders using and managing to the SOW must be convinced of its importance and value to their projects. Once these individuals are convinced that the SOW will help them manage their projects better and deliver those projects successfully, the document will essentially sell itself. As an organization gains more experience and maturity in developing and applying SOWs to its projects, the more successful those projects will be. From the perspective of a service provider, achieving this level of experience and maturity can be extremely important. Not only can a service provider sell the development of an SOW as a service offering, but it can also use the SOW as a vehicle to sell additional services.

The ultimate goals for every project manager and organization are to deliver all projects within their portfolio successfully—on-time, within budget, and of the quality desired by the client—and to achieve project excellence. **Achieving project excellence doesn't come free, and it doesn't come easy. It takes time, discipline, and the commitment of every member of the organization to make it happen.** Following the guidelines and methodologies presented throughout this book will help set you and your organization well on your way to achieving project excellence with the statement of work.

NOTE

[1] Rick Page, *Hope Is Not a Strategy: The 6 Keys to Winning the Complex Sale* (Atlanta: Nautilus Press, Inc., 2002).

Index

process, 34
size of change, impact of,
197–199
team members, poor
communication between,
206–207
understanding, lack of, 207
Change Order Request Form
Change Request Implementation
Decision, Section 4, 212
Change Request Information,
Section 2, 210–211
Change Request Investigation
Decision, Section 3, 211
Galaxy Telecommunications
statement of work example,
166
importance of, 208–209
Project Information, Section 1,
209–210
work instructions, 212–217
change order request number,
Change Order Request Form,
213–214
Change Order Tracker, 217–220
change-readiness effort, 47
changing priorities, as reason for
failed projects, 19
changing requirements, as reason
for failed projects, 19, 21
Chaos Report, 20–21
*Choate Construction v. Ideal Electrical
Contractors*, 201
Cleetus, Joseph, 44
client name, Change Order Request
Form, 214
client representative, TIGER team,
46
client satisfaction reports, statement
of work framework, 87
closeout, IT outsourcing project
phase, 43

coding structure, work breakdown
structure, 81–82
cohesion of team, relationship to
statement of work, 52–53
commitments, unrealistic, 17
Company USA, statement of work
example
assumptions, 174–175
attachments, 192–193
background information, 168–
169
billing process, 182
change control process, 180–181
constraints, 175
corporate responsibilities, 179
deliverables, 178
description, project management
maturity analysis, 176–177
description of work, 174
dispute resolution, 183
facilities/tools/equipment
requirements, 185–186
hours of operations, 184
introduction, 174–175
key assumptions, project
management maturity analysis,
177
management procedures, 180–
183
meetings, 182
pricing, 189–190
project management maturity
analysis, 176–178
purpose, 174
reports, 183
roles and responsibilities, 177–
178
sample reports, 193
schedule, 188
security requirements, 187
service pricing assumptions, 189
services provided, 176–178

Department of Defense (DOD)
Department of Defense Handbook—
Work Breakdown Structure
(MIL-HDBK-881), 68
guidelines for statement of work,
9, 11, 30
work breakdown structure, 68
Department of Motor Vehicles
(DMV), 22
description
Galaxy Telecommunications
statement of work example,
130, 133–134, 137–138
project management maturity
analysis, Company USA
statement of work example,
176–177
statement of work framework, 85
description of change request,
Change Order Request Form,
214
description of work
Company USA statement of
work example, 174
Galaxy Telecommunications
statement of work example,
126
statement of work framework,
83–84
design document, 10
developing, statement of work
framework, 78–79
development process, as service
offering, 229–230
discrepancy, 47
disposable camera, 45
dispute resolution
Company USA statement of
work example, 183
Galaxy Telecommunications
statement of work example, 147
statement of work framework, 87

DMV. *See* Department of Motor
Vehicles
DOD. *See* Department of Defense
due diligence
data, assembling and validating,
63–65
definition, 58
evaluation and control, 67
need for, 59
overlooking, 58
report, developing, 65–67
scope and purpose, defining,
60–61
selling importance of statement
of work to organization,
224–225
team, forming, 61–63

E

Eastman Kodak, 45
efficacy, 47
e-mail, 91
equipment requirements, statement
of work framework, 88–89
estimated cost to implement, Change
Order Request Form, 216
estimated cost to investigate,
Change Order Request Form,
214
estimated work effort to implement,
Change Order Request Form,
216
estimated work effort to investigate,
Change Order Request Form,
214
excitement, importance of, 224
executive steering committee,
Galaxy Telecommunications
statement of work example,
141–143
expectations
customer satisfaction and, 23–24

H

hardware support, Galaxy Telecommunications statement of work example, 133–136

hedging, in writing, 102–103

help desk services, Galaxy Telecommunications statement of work example, 130–133

Hilton, 22

historical perspective
early government contracting, 4–8
Noah's ark, 4
requirements documentation, 3–4

Hope Is Not a Strategy, 229

hours of operation
Company USA statement of work example, 184
Galaxy Telecommunications statement of work example, 149
statement of work framework, 87–88

I

impact of change on statement of work, Change Order Request Form, 215

implementation, IT outsourcing project phase, 43

incomplete requirements, as reason for failed projects, 19, 21

industry standards for statement of work, lack of, 11

information technology (IT)
outsourcing project phases, 43
projects, 20–21

instruction name, Change Order Request Form, 212

introduction
Company USA statement of work example, 174–175

Galaxy Telecommunications statement of work example, 125–128

statement of work framework, 83

investigation accepted, Change Order Request Form, 215

investigation rejected, Change Order Request Form, 215

IT. *See* information technology

J

jointly developed statement of work, 35

justification of change request, Change Order Request Form, 214

K

key assumptions
Company USA statement of work example, 177
Galaxy Telecommunications statement of work example, 131, 138
statement of work framework, 85

key requirements, statement of work framework, 86

L

lack of client input, as reason for failed projects, 19

lack of communication, 19

lack of executive support, as reason for failed projects, 19

lack of planning, as reason for failed projects, 19

lack of skilled resources, as reason for failed projects, 19

lack of user input, 21

legal department, baseline framework, obtaining approval of, 78

M

Maister, Dr. David, 23
management by objectives (MBO), 52
management procedures
  Company USA statement of work example, 180–183
  Galaxy Telecommunications statement of work example, 144–148
  statement of work framework, 87
Managing the Professional Service Firm, 23
marketing
  project phase, 43
  role of, 31
marketing group, when separate from sales group, 43
marketing requirements
  Galaxy Telecommunications statement of work example, 155
  statement of work framework, 91
Marriott, 22
Martin's Cone of Team Cohesion, 50–53
MBO. *See* management by objectives
meetings
  Company USA statement of work example, 182
  Galaxy Telecommunications statement of work example, 146
  statement of work framework, 87
Microsoft Project®, 73
MIL-HDBK-881. *See Department of Defense Handbook—Work Breakdown Structure*
Miorelli Engineering v. County of Brevard, 200
mismanaged projects, 18

misunderstandings, regarding statement of work, 30
mouse pads, 91

N

name of initiator, Change Order Request Form, 214
National Aeronautics and Space Administration (NASA)
  guidelines for statement of work, 9, 11, 30
  work breakdown structure, 68
needs assessment, 10
newsletters, 91
Noah's ark, 4
non-competitive bidding situations, when to develop statement of work, 34–35, 38–39
nonspecific words, in writing, 104–106

O

OBS. *See* organizational breakdown structure
Occupational Safety and Health Act of 1970, 89
open-ended phrases, in writing, 106
operation and maintenance, IT outsourcing project phase, 43
Oregon Department of Motor Vehicles, 22
organizational breakdown structure (OBS), 72
origination, of projects, 30

P

Page, Rick, 229
PARIS method, for assigning responsibilities, 62
penalties and bonuses, Galaxy Telecommunications statement of work example, 159–160

PERT. *See* Program Evaluation Review Technique
pharmaceutical projects, 21
phrases having multiple meanings, in writing, 101
planning and design, IT outsourcing project phase, 43
PM. *See* project manager
PMBOK®. *See* Project Management Body of Knowledge
PMI®. *See* Project Management Institute
Polaris Weapon System, 68
poor documentation, 19
poor writing, 19
positive words, in writing, 95, 98
posters, 91
Post-it® Notes method, 73
Power of the Penny, 197–198
PR. *See* purchase request
precedence diagram, work breakdown structure, 72
preparation, statement of work, 8–9
price, 108
pricing
  Company USA statement of work example, 189–190
  Galaxy Telecommunications statement of work example, 157–160
  model, 108–110
  statement of work framework, 89
private sector projects, 9
process steps, Change Order Request Form, 213–217
process user or executioner, Change Order Request Form, 217
procurement process, requirement for statement of work, 30
product responsibility transfer, statement of work framework, 90

products provided, statement of work framework, 85–86
professional services assembly line, 43–44
professional services industry, need for statement of work, 10–12
profitability, 200
Program Evaluation Review Technique (PERT), 68
program manager, 70
project charter, 10
project complexity, 9
project failures
  impact, 18–19
  reasons for, 19
  statement of work, relationship to, 15
Project Information, Change Order Request Form, 209–210
Project Management Body of Knowledge (PMBOK®), 11
Project Management Institute (PMI®), 11
project management maturity analysis, 176–178
project manager (PM)
  assigning to due diligence team, 61–62
  Change Order Request Form, 214
  toothpaste syndrome, 17
  use of statement of work, 9–10
  work breakdown structure, 69
project name, Change Order Request Form, 214
project number, Change Order Request Form, 214
project recovery team, 19
projects, origination of, 30
proposal statement of work (PSOW)
  competitive bidding situations, 34

sample reports
  Company USA statement of
    work example, 193
  Galaxy Telecommunications
    statement of work example,
    167
schedule
  balancing with scope and cost,
    199–200
  Company USA statement of
    work example, 188
  Galaxy Telecommunications
    statement of work example,
    156
  overruns, 200
  statement of work framework, 89
  work breakdown structure,
    relationship to, 72
scope creep, as reason for failed
  projects, 19, 200
scope of work
  balancing with cost and schedule,
    199–200
  compared to statement of work, 10
  unrealistic, 17
scope statement, Change Order
  Request Form, 212
security requirements
  Company USA statement of
    work example, 187
  Galaxy Telecommunications
    statement of work example,
    154
  statement of work framework, 90
selling importance of statement of
  work
  to clients, 227–229
  to organization, 224–227
service level agreement (SLA)
  Galaxy Telecommunications
    statement of work example,
    132–133, 135–136, 139–140

importance of, 86
  statement of work framework, 86
service pricing assumptions
  Company USA statement of
    work example, 189
  Galaxy Telecommunications
    statement of work example,
    157–158
service responsibility transfer
  Galaxy Telecommunications
    statement of work example,
    153
  statement of work framework, 90
services provided
  Company USA statement of
    work example, 176–178
  Galaxy Telecommunications
    statement of work example,
    130–140
  statement of work framework,
    85–86
shipping fees
  Company USA statement of
    work example, 190
  Galaxy Telecommunications
    statement of work example,
    159
signature block
  Company USA statement of
    work example, 191
  Galaxy Telecommunications
    statement of work example,
    161
  statement of work framework, 89
simple language, in writing, 95
skills, absence of, 17
SLA. *See* service level agreement
SME. *See* subject matter expert
software support, Galaxy
  Telecommunications statement of
  work example, 137–140
sole-source provider, 34

sovereign immunity doctrine, 201
SOW. *See* statement of work
standard hardware component list,
    Galaxy Telecommunications
    statement of work example, 164
standard software application list,
    Galaxy Telecommunications
    statement of work example, 164
Standish Group International,
    20–21
statement of confidentiality
    Company USA statement of
        work example, 173
    Galaxy Telecommunications
        statement of work example,
        124
statement of work framework, 83
statement of work (SOW),
    importance of, 1–2
status reports, statement of work
    framework, 87
steady-state delivery team, 43
subject matter expert (SME), 42,
    44, 61
superlatives, in writing, 107
Supreme Court of Florida, 200

T

table of contents (TOC)
    Company USA statement of
        work example, 171–172
    Galaxy Telecommunications
        statement of work example,
        122–123
    statement of work framework, 82
tasks, parallel compared to
    sequential, 44
team members
    cohesion, importance of, 51
    developing statement of work,
        34, 41
technical language, in writing, 98

telecommunications projects, 21
termination fees
    Company USA statement of
        work example, 190
    Galaxy Telecommunications
        statement of work example,
        159
terms and conditions (Ts & Cs), 78,
    111
terms of art, in writing, 103–104
theory of quantum meruit, 201
TIGER team. *See* Totally
    Integrated Groups of Expert
    Resources team
time and materials
    Company USA statement of
        work example, 189
    Galaxy Telecommunications
        statement of work example,
        158–159
TOC. *See* table of contents
tool requirements, Change Order
    Request Form, 213
tools, statement of work framework,
    88
toothpaste syndrome, 17
Totally Integrated Groups of Expert
    Resources (TIGER) team
    benefits of using, 48
    collocation of team members,
        49–50
    communication, 50
    definition, 45–46
    due diligence team, relationship
        to, 61–62
    identifying resources, 48–49
    requirements for implementing,
        47
    resource-intensive nature, 47–48
    size, 49
    subject matter experts, selecting,
        49

Management Concepts, Inc.
Project Management Titles

▶ **Essentials of Software Project Management**
Richard Bechtold, PhD

▶ **Fast Forms for Managing Software Projects**
Kathleen A. Demery, PMP, and Monica Lusk

▶ **IT Project Management Handbook**
Jag Sodhi and Prince Sodhi

▶ **Project Management Essential Library**

Managing Project Integration
Denis F. Cioffi, PhD

Managing Projects for Value
John C. Goodpasture, PMP

Effective Work Breakdown Structures
Gregory T. Haugan, PhD, PMP

Project Planning and Scheduling
Gregory T. Haugan, PhD, PMP

Managing Project Quality
Timothy J. Kloppenborg, PhD, PMP, and Joseph A. Petrick, PhD, SPHR

Project Leadership
Timothy J. Kloppenborg, PhD, PMP, Art Shriberg, MEd EdD,
    and Jayashree Venkatraman, MS, MBA

Project Measurement
Steve Neuendorf

Project Estimating and Cost Management
Parviz F. Rad, PhD

Project Risk Management
Paul S. Royer

- **People Skills for Project Managers**
  Steven W. Flannes, PhD, and Ginger Levin, DPA
- **Powerful Project Leadership**
  Wayne Strider
- **E-Learning Series**

  PM Power Trac

  Project Planning and Scheduling Trainer

Visit our website at www.managementconcepts.com
Or call us at (800) 506-4450